The Way of the Owl

The Way of the Owl

Succeeding with Integrity in a Conflicted World

Frank Rivers

HarperSanFrancisco
An Imprint of HarperCollins*Publishers*

HarperSanFrancisco and the author, in association with The Basic Foundation, a not-for-profit organization whose primary mission is reforestation, will facilitate the planting of two trees for every one tree used in the manufacture of this book.

A TREE CLAUSE BOOK

The author gratefully acknowledges the following for permission to reprint previously published material: Columbia University Press for lines from *Chuang Tzu*. Translated by Burton Watson. Copyright © 1964 by Columbia University Press. Reprinted with permission of the publisher. The Overlook Press for *A Book of Five Rings* by Miyamoto Musashi. Translated by Victor Harris. Copyright © 1974 by Victor Harris. Published by The Overlook Press, Woodstock, NY 12498. Used by permission. Simon & Schuster for an excerpt from *The Analects of Confucius*, translated by Arthur Waley. Copyright ©1938 by George Allen & Unwin Ltd. Reprinted by permission.

HarperCollins Web Site: http://www.harpercollins.com

HarperCollins®, ■®, HarperSanFrancisco™, and A TREE CLAUSE BOOK®
are trademarks of HarperCollins Publishers.

FIRST EDITION
Book design by Ralph Fowler

Library of Congress Cataloging-in-Publication Data
    Rivers, Frank.
    The way of the owl : succeeding with integrity in a conflicted world / Frank Rivers.
    ISBN 0–06–251207–2 (cloth)
    ISBN 0–06–251397–4 (pbk.)
    1. Adjustment (Psychology)   2. Adaptability (Psychology)
    3. Conflict (Psychology)   I. Title.
    BF335.R5   1996
    155.2'4—dc20   95–20645

    96 97 98 99 00 ❖ RRDH 10 9 8 7 6 5 4 3

*Whosoever knows how to fight well
is not angry.
Whosoever knows how to conquer
enemies does not fight them.*

LAO TZU, TAO TE CHING

*A man who strikes first admits that
his ideas have given out.*

CHINESE PROVERB

I rejoice that there are owls.

HENRY DAVID THOREAU

Contents

The Way of the Owl

The Bird of Wisdom

*But ah! if we could perceive the world of the owl, what strange
sounds and beautiful forms we might enjoy!*

ROBERT W. NERO, *Phantom of the Northern Forest*

Behold the fledgling. An awkward creature, his life is marked by anxiety, resistance, and struggle. He staggers from one activity to the next, sometimes taking flight, other times crashing into obstacles. On most days, he is unaware of his surroundings and the consequences of his actions. He has a narrow comfort zone and is confused about his priorities. His attention is unstable and fragmented, he ignores the lessons of the natural world, and he thinks in black and white. When he meets resistance, he overreacts with aggression or underreacts with passivity. Arguments and misunderstandings interfere with his work, frustrate him, and make him vulnerable.

Sadly, the fledgling has received little training for life in a conflicted, competitive world. He has no idea why people fight with one another or how conflict might be put to creative use. No one has ever told him how to move with grace and effectiveness. No one has ever taught him how to deal with the other side of a difficult and acrimonious relationship. Naive and confused, he lives with the belief that there are only two ways to touch the world around him: the passive, yielding behavior of the dove or the strong, aggressive way of the hawk. He tries these approaches, but finds himself frustrated, either creating chaos and violence or becoming a victim.

Fortunately, the fledgling need not struggle forever. There is a better way. It is possible to strike a balance between passivity and aggression, perform well in conflict, and create productive relationships without being victimized. The knowledge does exist. It is the way of the owl.

For the ancients, the owl united the virtues of knowledge and wisdom. Legend has it that an owl nested in the pillars of the Acropolis, the temple dedicated to the goddess Athena. The Athenians admired the owl's eyes—those large, gleaming orbs that stared down from the nest high in the Acropolis. They believed that the very brilliance of those eyes provided an inner light that enabled the owl to see clearly in the dark of night. At least one Greek general kept a trained owl on hand, ready to release whenever its circling presence might make the difference between victory and defeat.

In fact, the owl is a master of flight and adaptation. The product of forty million years of evolution, he is a superb animal, integrating intelligence, power, grace, and beauty. He takes a variety of inspirational forms, from the shy and retiring flammulated owl to the awesome predatory power of the great horned owl. In all cases, the owl is acutely aware and adaptive. He routinely varies his behavior and defensive strategies to adjust to changing conditions. He is flexible in his feeding habits and nest-building choices. He varies his territories to fit food supplies and population densities. His vision and hearing are outstanding. In this, the owl makes a perfect model for mastery. Owls have much to teach us about living in a conflicted and ever-changing world. We would be wise to attend to them.

Similarly, the owlish human is a creature of many skills. She has a rich repertoire of skills and orientations that give her versatility in conflict. She is a master of sensitivity, dialogue, and physical presence. She is balanced, poised, and graceful under pressure. She is capable of perfect stillness as well as decisive action.

The human owl is a creature of great martial intelligence, well versed in the arts of strategy and conflict resolution. Never a victim, never an aggressor, she takes the middle path between hawk and dove. She is highly skilled at fighting, but is also adept at not fighting. She can defend herself from attack, but she can also create understanding, calm disagreements, and promote ecological relationships; she is a warrior as well as an anti-warrior. Because she understands the principles of engagement and tactics, she can operate effectively in all realms of conflicted relationship.

Her study is both broad and deep. It includes the arts of strategy, language, clear thinking, and integration. It is about survival and adaptation, balance and proportion, attention and awareness. It is about knowing one's self, one's environment, and one's opponent. It is about risk and mastery.

The path to owlhood is simple yet elusive and demanding. When you take this path, you will find yourself challenged by a new way of living and relating. You will meet resistance and you will struggle. Nevertheless, you will ultimately be rewarded. As you become increasingly adept, you will feel liberated and empowered by new options and alternatives. You will feel less vulnerable to attack and will find yourself penetrating to the core of experience and meaning. You will begin to move with poise, grace, and effectiveness.

Prepare yourself for sustained effort. Each one of us has the potential for owlish mastery, but this is a potential that must be nurtured. This is a lifetime undertaking.

CHAPTER ONE

Priorities

Swing a Sharp Blade

It is to no purpose, it is even against one's own interest,
to turn away from the real nature of the affair because
the horror of its elements excites repugnance.

Carl von Clausewitz, *On War*

Before beginning the path to owlhood, the fledgling must come to grips with martial knowledge; he must think about fighting itself. Like it or not, fighting is an integral part of human experience. It is crucial that we face the beast.

Some would prefer to avoid the study of martial knowledge altogether and concentrate instead on peaceful arts, but conflict and harmony are really two ends of the same stick. To understand one, you must understand the other. Some knowledge of fighting is essential to all successful relationship. Therefore you must study the dynamics of force and fraud, the psychology of conflict, and the strategies that lead to victory and defeat. You must learn how to fight well, especially if you desire harmony. Avoidance is a double trap: not only will you fail to make peace, but you will also become victimized in the process. As the saying goes, "You may not be interested in fighting, but fighting is surely interested in you."

Martial knowledge is an edged tool, a mental blade. As with all edged tools, a sharp blade is safer and more effective. Because he fails to study the nature of conflict and strategy, the fledgling wields a dull and dangerous blade. He thinks that he is safe, but in fact the opposite is true. His actions require more force, and if the dull blade slips, he injures himself and those around him. His partial understanding makes him dangerous, vulnerable, and ineffective.

Our troubles with fighting do not come from martial knowledge. Rather, they come from a *lack* of martial knowledge. Ignorance and denial are always errors. Denying the possibility of a fight is one of the easiest ways of getting involved in one. Ignorance is never a safe place. The only security lies in knowledge. The only benevolence lies in training.

Embrace Enmity

A warrior cannot complain or regret anything. His life
is an endless challenge, and challenges cannot possibly be
good or bad. Challenges are simply challenges.

Carlos Castaneda, *Tales of Power*

Above all, the fledgling wants to be safe. Conflict makes him anxious,
and so he avoids it whenever possible. He believes that if he is nice to
everyone, he will never make enemies or be attacked. He sees no reason why anyone should oppose him. After all, he is simply being reasonable. So he redoubles his efforts and dismisses his enemies as strange
aberrations. Perhaps the people who oppose him are crazy, ignorant,
or evil.

The owl is under no such illusions. He appreciates the broad scope
of human values, worldviews, and interests. With diversity comes conflict and resistance. Even the nicest of the nice will meet opposition,
sometimes stubborn, furious, and violent. This is inevitable.

Conflict is woven into the fabric of all life; opposition is normal.
Reasonable creatures disagree with each other all the time. No matter
what you do, someone will find it controversial. Action always pro-
vokes criticism. Truly creative acts antagonize; innovation is always a
threat to the established order. The only way to avoid enmity is to do
nothing, say nothing, and be nothing; but this is the path to irrele-
vance, not owlhood.

Fighting fighting is a waste of time and energy. No matter how
great your skill, you will still meet resistance and opposition in your
life. No one, not even the most accomplished and sophisticated owl,
can avoid conflicted relationships. To desire freedom from enmity is to

desire separation from life itself; this is like an attempt to escape breathing. Ultimately, the only solution is acceptance.

Do not be surprised when you encounter resistance. Meet it with grace and skill. By embracing the reality of enmity, you will be liberated from illusion. Opposition will no longer disturb your balance, and your performance will flow uninterrupted by internal resistance. Best of all, you will have one less enemy to fight.

Be a Good Animal

Hold fast to the great primal image.

Lao Tzu, *Tao te Ching*

It is therefore necessary for the prince to know
well how to use both the beast and the man.

Machiavelli, *The Prince*

The owl is a superb animal, a master of physical presence, grace, and alertness. She relishes physical reality and takes delight in sensation and movement. She lives in her body and listens to the music of her own metabolism. She feels the waxing and waning of the living energy that pulsates in every cell.

The vibrant animal body responds creatively and appropriately to conflict challenges. The healthy animal is capable of sustained physical challenge, ambiguity tolerance, and delayed gratification, key ingredients in all creative performance. In contrast, the fledgling ignores his body; he lives in a fog of somatic apathy. In failing to provide for his animal nature, he becomes passive, violent, ineffective, and vulnerable; he loses his artistry.

This is an art of relationship. Your body is your first, last, and most vital ally—the source of all your power. Strengthen this alliance at every opportunity. Challenge your tissue regularly, but do not punish it. Never treat your animal body as an adversary, for this is one battle that you will surely lose.

Find out what your animal nature needs and provide it; become a master of self-care. The animal body needs fresh air, fresh water, high-quality food, regular movement, and touch. Master the somatic fundamentals: walking, breathing, and being still. Listen to your cellular intelligence; trust the homeostatic wisdom of your tissue: Eat when hungry, drink when thirsty, sleep when tired.

Breathe deeply and intentionally. Your breath is an exceptionally wise teacher, for each phase of inhalation and exhalation is a simultaneous combination of power and relaxation, yin and yang. Study this movement with full expression at every opportunity. Breathe with each cell and every fiber of your animal body.

Intensify your animal presence. The body of the good animal is well-aligned, flexible, alert, and dignified. This is essential to all levels of relationship and combat. In perfect posture, prime movers and antagonists alternate in a dance of contraction and release. The body is rooted in the ground and yet light and flexible in the head and neck. Here the owl creates a balanced relationship with gravity, neither fighting it excessively nor conceding to its pull. This art is a combination of strength and release that requires attention, sincerity, and periodic adjustment.

The language of the body speaks to the unconscious of others and is thus extremely powerful. Other creatures react strongly to the way we stand, sit, and walk. Rarely will an aggressor attack a person who looks alert, capable, and aligned; the thug wants a target who is slumped and contracted or brazen and challenging. Study the varieties of human and animal posture that you see around you and imitate those that work.

A rigid animal body is not well-suited to conflict artistry. Tension inhibits our skills; we lose our grace, power, sensitivity, and humor. Therefore the owlish animal learns the art of release, a subtle skill of paradox and counterintuition: The fledgling cannot relax because he feels vulnerable and afraid, but the owl knows that relaxation is precisely the path to safety.

This principle is well illustrated by an ancient Chinese kite-fighting game. Players coated kite strings with ground glass, floated the kites aloft, and then maneuvered them, trying to cut the opponent's string. The taut string is more easily cut; the string that is yielding and nonresistant is safe. The message is clear: The tense and rigid are defeated, while the soft and pliable endure. Practice this art of nonresistance. Reverse your effort to absorb the opposition.

The good animal cycles her behavior between challenge and pampering. She exposes her body to the rigors of the environment and then nurtures it in healing. Seek a state of dynamic balance at all levels of somatic relationship. Honor the yang channel of physical activation—fight and flight. Honor the yin channel of rejuvenation, healing and recovery. Vigorous action and training are fundamental to be sure, but some degree of sloth is also essential. The key is balance; alternate purposeful action with periods of deep and intentional rest.

In caring for your animal health, emphasize preemption and prevention. Do not procrastinate in meeting the needs of the animal body. If you become sick or injured, address your condition with vigorous countermeasures and grateful acceptance simultaneously. To treat injury and illness strictly as adversaries to be defeated will only increase internal conflict and make healing less likely. Pain is valuable feedback and thus an ally; pain teaches. Heed the message that your body provides or suffer the consequences.

All creatures have lessons to teach. Some have tremendous power, others mobility and stealth. All can adapt. Can you endure winter with the stoic nature of a grizzly bear? Move with the power and grace of the mountain lion? Adapt with the skill of a chameleon? Navigate with the precision of a migratory bird? See with the visual acuity of the owl? Fire your imagination with images of the biological world.

The ultimate key to animalhood is exposure. In a misguided attempt at self-protection, the fledgling insulates himself from the natural world. The animal body cannot live in isolation, however; it must touch the wild earth to remain healthy. Knowing this, the owl exposes herself to her environment; she makes herself vulnerable to the lessons of land, sea, and sky. Do not neglect this practice. Spend the night out in the mountains or the desert. Fast. Walk farther than you think you can. Dive into cold water. Keep the animal alive, alert, and vibrant.

Expand Your Comfort Zone

Study the Ways of all professions.

Miyamoto Musashi, *A Book of Five Rings*

There is only one subject matter for education,
and that is Life in all its manifestations.

Alfred North Whitehead, *The Aims of Education*

The owl is a highly adaptable bird, well-suited to a wide diversity of habitats ranging from deep forests to desert cliffs, from wetlands to high mountains. He roosts in dense foliage, tree holes, old nests, and cliff ledges, as well as on open ground. He eats a diverse fare that includes everything from insects to mice, gophers, salamanders, birds, fish, beetles, and scorpions. The owl has a wide comfort zone.

There is a close relationship between an animal's comfort zone and his ability to stay alive. The basic rule is simple: The wider the comfort zone, the greater the chances of survival. The animal who is only comfortable on a mild summer day will be severely challenged if he is forced to spend a night out in the mountains in the winter. If he is adapted to a life of inactivity, he will find it difficult to run away from a hostile attacker.

The comfort zone begins within the animal body, where we become accustomed to patterns of movement and sensation. Similarly, we also find comfort in social, cultural, political, and ideological dimensions. We live in linguistic comfort zones, spiritual comfort zones, and intellectual comfort zones. We try to surround ourselves with people who think like we do, people who read the same books and hold the same values.

An expanded comfort zone benefits the owl in a number of ways. First, it makes him a good fighter. Ample experience helps him tolerate higher levels of adversity, pain, and ambiguity while maintaining his composure and intelligence. An expanded comfort zone also increases his range of tactical options. Wider experience gives him the latitude to move and create. This in turn allows a greater sense of control, confidence, and objectivity.

Remember, conflicted relationships follow no laws. Every opponent is unique, every attack fundamentally unpredictable. Even the most visionary owl cannot know in advance how a conflict will develop or what he might have to do to defend himself. Therefore the owl refuses to rely on any single technique or discipline. He knows that *any* knowledge is potentially useful. *All* paths have some value. Knowing this, the owl attempts to learn as many arts as possible. He develops a rich repertoire.

Do not reject any form of knowledge! Do not place arbitrary limits on what may be useful. Be an opportunist—soak up knowledge whenever and wherever possible. All ideas are potentially valuable, not only for practical self-defense and survival, but also as a source of metaphor, creative inspiration, and relationship building. As your knowledge base grows, so will your network of relationships. This leads to empathy, compassion, and understanding. Above all, seek versatility. Learn to play multiple roles. Become a student of many disciplines. A broad base of knowledge is always a no-lose proposition.

Be a xenophile; embrace the different and the unusual as a matter of course. When poised on the cusp of decision, go toward your fear, anxiety, and incompetence. Seek out new experiences for their own sake and intentionally expose yourself to novelty.

Expand your linguistic comfort zone by learning new words. Expand your psychological comfort zone by exposing yourself to new ideas. Meet new people; learn new rituals and myths. Move your body in new ways.

It will help you if your training is specific to the challenges you are likely to face, but expanding your comfort zone in *any* dimension is valuable because it will make you familiar with novelty and the process of adaptation. Any new experience will enhance your performance and survivability.

The process is invariably threatening and intimidating. Leaving the security of our physical, social, and psychological nest requires that we face risk, uncertainty, and ambiguity. Nevertheless, the effort is crucial. Human comfort zones follow the familiar "use it or lose it" principle. If you don't challenge the limits from time to time, your comfort zone will actually begin to shrink. This is not the way of the owl.

Don't Get Hit

Travel where there is no enemy.

Sun Tzu, *The Art of War*

The owl is a pacifist, but she is not a passivist. She seeks peace, but does not allow herself to become a victim. She is not deceived by well-intended martial philosophies that claim passivity as the way to peaceful relationship. On the contrary, she knows that she can't do any creative work if she is abused, victimized, or dead. Like all good animals, she defends her niche in the ecosystem.

There are several ways to avoid the physical and psychological strike. The first is simply not to be there when the attacker makes his move. This art begins with awareness—the owl extends her intelligence deep into her environment. She avoids dangerous situations and takes up positions of relative safety. She uses her superior judgment to avoid situations that would require the use of her superior skill. If she's not there, she won't be hit.

Of course, the owl is a fallible creature—sometimes she *is* there when the attack occurs. At this point, the best option may be evasion. Retreat may be necessary as well as honorable. Or it may be possible to avoid the strike by getting off the line of attack. Instead of defending a static position, the owl sidesteps the incoming strike without advance or retreat.

This art demands flexibility and a willingness to abandon position. Physically, it requires balance and agility. Psychologically, it demands a fluid and mobile mind. When verbally assaulted, the owl does not counter the accusation directly, nor does she passively accept it; she takes a lateral step, an alternative view.

The fledgling does not comprehend this lesson. When conflict breaks out, she defends her stance and hardens her position. As conflict intensifies, she adds additional levels of defense and roots herself firmly in one spot. Ultimately, she loses her maneuverability just when she needs it most.

In all cases, mobility is essential. Don't be a static target. Stay relaxed, centered, and fluid. Above all, do not become hypnotized by the attack. Continue to scan your environment comprehensively, looking for other attacks, openings in your opponent's defense, and other creative possibilities. Honor the attack, as you must; but don't allow it to tyrannize your attention or your intelligence.

Because of her superior mobility, the owl can also choose to blend with the attack and redirect it. In this case, she adjusts her position and motion so that it closely parallels that of her attacker. Once her behavior is in harmony with her opponent, she is not only safer, but is also in a position to direct his momentum.

Imagine a boulder rolling down a hill. If you try to stop it with direct force or dogged resistance, you will be defeated. But if you run up alongside it and give it a nudge in a new direction, you will remain safe. Metaphorically, this approach holds the potential for a mutually beneficial outcome in which neither party is injured.

The fledgling misunderstands blending to be weak and ineffective, but, in fact, a well-executed blend can be devastating. Since it harnesses the attacker's energy and momentum, redirection comes as a complete surprise and the attacker, in a sense, throws himself. There is nothing passive or weak about this art. A blend may appear nonresistant or feel soft, but this is simply a means to a creative end. The owl may yield, but she continues to maintain integrity while making precise adjustments in position and movement. She keeps contact with her interests and objectives even as she yields. She loses to win. She gives in to get her way.

Before you can blend and redirect an attack, you must know where it is coming from and where it is going. In hand-to-hand combat, this is superficially obvious, but in general practice, most attacks are ambiguous. A harsh word or a rude gesture may not be what it appears. Thus you must observe your opponent with sensitivity. Get inside his experience and find out what he really wants.

This is a highly paradoxical art, but the benefits are enormous. Once you see through the eyes of your adversary, your blend will be more complete and effective. With knowledge, you can move parallel with the flow and make small corrections to its course. If you execute skillfully, you can make the necessary adjustments to the attack without putting yourself or your opponent at excessive risk.

There are related benefits as well. As you blend with your opponent's attack, you may come to see that his view is really not so irrational, unjustified, or immoral after all. This may resolve the conflict with no further effort. Paradoxically, a strategy aimed at victory may eventually lead to mutual understanding and peaceful coexistence. Embrace this possibility.

Learn the Art of Falling

I get up. I walk. I fall down.
Meanwhile, I keep dancing.

Rabbi Hillel

When falling, dive.

Unknown

Even the most highly skilled conflict artist will occasionally lose his balance, overextend his reach, or get distracted. He may miss a block, underestimate his opponent, or fail to set limits. At some point in his life, he will be thrown, either literally or metaphorically. He will take a fall.

The owl is well aware of this possibility. As a fallible creator, he knows that all of his behaviors, methods, assumptions, and conclusions are potentially mistaken. Therefore he trains himself to fall gracefully. He learns to make smooth transitions through the unexpected and back to a state of dynamic balance. In this art, a fall made gracefully is scarcely a fall at all, merely a transition.

The psychological art mirrors the physical. In the physical fall, excess rigidity means broken limbs, but excess yielding leads to traumatized joints and torn tissue. Thus successful ground contact consists of balanced physical concentration; simultaneously strong and yielding, hard and soft. The owlish athlete doesn't fight the ground, but he doesn't allow it to punish him either.

The key element in this art is your relationship with error. If you accept mistakes and poor judgment too readily, your performance will stagnate. If you see error as an adversary, you will become rigid and inflexible—and more likely to take the fall that you were trying to avoid in the first place. If you war too strongly against error, you will never be able to enter the flow of peak performance. As usual, the optimal relationship is paradoxical. For the owl, errors are both foe and ally.

When you trip, physically or metaphorically, acknowledge your error at the earliest possible instant, compensate as gracefully as you can, and return to your original objective. This is the art of falling.

Anything can happen in a conflict encounter. All may go as planned, or the relationship might shift in an entirely novel direction. Therefore you must create alternates for every expectation and an exit strategy for every engagement. Never assume that your tactics will get the result you intended.

Unfortunately, many of us resist revision. We have time and ego invested in our original plans, and so we cling to them. But the more you resist revision, the harder you will fall. Errors and inadequacies of the original plan will multiply over time. Eventually it will collapse entirely and you will be hurled to the ground.

The owlish alternative is to embrace the fallibility of all human enterprises. Recognize your original plan as an ideal that is totally at the mercy of reality. It is almost certainly flawed in some way. Do not be surprised when it fails to live up to its promise. Expect it.

There is no failure here. Your alternate plan is likely to be more appropriate and more aesthetic than the original. The purpose of the original plan was to give some direction, however rough, to your actions. Its demise is nothing to grieve over. Simply replace it with the alternate and continue. The mastery lies in transition.

Of course, as soon as you adopt your alternate, you will need to adjust for its inevitable errors as well. Graceful falling consists of making a smooth transition from original to alternate, then creating a new alternate and a new transition. The process is open-ended.

For the owl, disruption is not only acceptable, it is also essential. Observe the way that apparently catastrophic events contribute to the health of all ecosystems. Just as wildfire, hurricanes, and drought keep natural systems in a state of productive flux, so too does error reset the creative life of the owlish artist. Do not suppress these events! Allow the wildfires to burn in your experience and regenerate your creative powers. Honor your failures.

The fledgling finds this talk of falling and retreat to be distracting and even dishonorable; he believes that it shows a lack of spirit and confidence. The owl, however, knows otherwise. Planning for failure and retreat is a simple act of intelligence that honors the unpredictable nature of the universe. If there is dishonor, it is in flying off unaware and oblivious to danger.

CHAPTER TWO

Creative Maneuver and Relationship

First Principle:
The Enemy Is Never Wrong

"Wish" and "want" trip the feet,
but "is" makes the path smoother.

Wisdom of the Aes Sedai
Robert Jordan, *The Fires of Heaven*

The owl's wisdom is based on the principle that, no matter how an enemy behaves, he can never be wrong. Whether he casts verbal insults, grabs us by the lapels, sticks a knife in our ribs, or files an outrageous lawsuit, it makes no difference: The enemy just is.

The fledgling, of course, denies this proposition outright. She gets angry and upset when she meets resistance. She curses her adversaries and whines about their unreasonable behavior.

This is a poor use of intelligence. The fledgling's complaints about her opponent's behavior may be accurate, but they are also irrelevant. Like it or not, resistance is a fact of life. Whatever an opponent does, no matter how immoral, unjust, or illegal, is the artist's medium. This is the material we have to work with.

Realizing this, the owl accepts whatever attack comes her way and responds with grace. Adversaries are capable of all kinds of behaviors—some rational, some bizarre. The owl's task is not to judge or moralize on the correctness of her enemy's behavior, but to respond with creativity and intelligence.

In a fight, any behavior is possible and, in a way, acceptable. An assailant's attack, whether it be verbal or physical, aggressive or subtle, just *is*. Your disapproval is irrelevant; what matters is the quality of your response.

Extend this principle beyond the realm of hand-to-hand combat to any resistance you may encounter. Make the enemy a model for life.

In this, your predicament is never wrong; your predicament just *is*. Your environment is never wrong; your environment just *is*. Your state of health is never wrong. Your government is never wrong. Your partner is never wrong.

Give up your resistance to resistance. Engage the enemy as you find him, not as you wish him to be. Once you embody this principle, you will realize an instant and dramatic improvement in your performance. When you abandon the inertia of analysis and judgment, you will no longer be stuck. You will remain fluid, active, and alert.

Mind with Matter

O, it is excellent
To have a giant's strength, but it is tyrannous
To use it like a giant.

Shakespeare

For the aspiring owl, the foundation relationship upon which all others depend begins with the physical universe. There can be no mastery without competence at this level.

In his experience with the physical, the fledgling attempts to exercise crude control. He seeks mind over matter, or more accurately, mind against matter. In this relationship, the fledgling's tools are force, power, and control; always a bigger hammer. His relationship is adversarial and dissonant.

This approach is doomed to eventual failure. In a war between mind and matter, matter will eventually win. The best that the fledgling can hope for is a sporadic sort of control that alternates between rigid dominance and unexpected, catastrophic failure.

Alternately, the fledgling may succumb passively, surrendering power or control. In this case, he puts mind *under* matter, and is swept downstream by the current of circumstance and events. This course is also guaranteed to fail.

The only possible solution is a harmonious meshing of mind with matter, a cooperative union. Here the artist's mind blends with matter and exercises partial, provisional control. The tools are sensitivity, attention, and insight. This is a path of gentle persuasion and intelligent power, never brute force.

Study the materials you use and honor their nature. Whether they be wood, metal, paper, or cloth, adapt your touch to them. Exercise control and manipulation as necessary, but only in harmony with their essential qualities. Become one with the medium. Be strong with the heavy, gentle with the delicate, and graceful with the awkward.

Last Things First

Not having a goal is worse
than not reaching one.

Schuler

The owl does not simply take wing at random. Before she takes flight, she knows where she is going and why. The objectives she selects provide a point of focus, a touchstone on which she can depend in the midst of chaos. These objectives bring an essential sense of order to her attention and prevent her from leaping impulsively.

Since we live in a world of flux, our targets are usually moving. A static objective will soon be irrelevant or dangerous. A wise objective today might be a fool's goal tomorrow. Perfect accuracy on the wrong target is a waste of time and skill. Consequently, the owl updates objectives continuously and does not become obsessed by the first bull's-eye she has selected.

Vague targets are notoriously hard to hit—abstractions don't give feedback. You will never know if you hit the targets of "peace," "security," or "happiness." Therefore the owl wields her imagination with precision. She works on specific detail, constantly seeking the finer points of your objectives. The opportunity for success lies in the modest and attainable.

The quality of our objectives is shaped by our perceptions. Consider the fledgling. When he encounters resistance, he calls it a "problem" and tries to "solve" it with strategies, tactics, or technologies. His relationship is negative, reactive, and adversarial.

In contrast, the owl begins with an image of something she would like to bring into being; she lives on the cutting edge of creativity. This approach is positive, active, and growth–oriented. Because she concentrates on bringing her vision into being, many of the "problems" that plague the fledgling never appear. In taking this creative path, the owl transcends problems by reaching beyond them.

Because of her superior experience, the owl is inclined to see conflicted relationships not as problems or obstacles, but as opportunities for creative expression. Instead of focusing on something she would like to get rid of, she concentrates on something she would like to bring into being. Instead of opposing conflict, the owl embraces its inherent value. Each encounter with resistance offers an opportunity for education, beauty, meaning, and value.

Both the problem-solving and the creative approaches are valuable parts of the owl's repertoire. Have no doubt on this score—a sharp knife held to the throat is a distinct problem that should be solved as quickly as possible. Ultimately, however, the owl is more interested in creativity than in solving problems. Remember, the musician does not see sound as a problem. The painter does not see color as a problem. The dancer does not see movement as a problem. On the contrary, these artists see opportunities for creative engagement.

Come to grips with the problems that need to be solved, but don't get bogged down in the process. Reach beyond the problem to the vision of what you are trying to create. Exercise a synthesis; work on problems and visions simultaneously. Do not be distracted by the irritations and annoyances of the things you don't want; create a vision of what you do want and pursue it with passion.

Go to the Source

For the fledgling, most conflicts are vague, shadowy affairs. He struggles like a boxer in the dark, battling against unknown forces. He stumbles awkwardly and wastes his creative energy, unsure of where the opposition truly lies. The owl, on the other hand, identifies his opposition with clarity and precision. He goes directly to the root of resistance.

In some cases, the situation is clear. If a stranger assaults you on the street, you can be sure who your opponent is. But in many instances, resistance is ambiguous. The fledgling assumes that the person who makes him mad is the opponent, but this may be an error; the more significant resistance may be somewhere else altogether. Frequently, our conflict challenges are complex webs of projection, misunderstanding, and failed communication. In cases like these, the owlish question is not only "*Who* is the opponent?" but also "*What* is the opponent?" The problem may not be a person, but a personality; not an individual, but an attitude; not an organization, but a policy.

Focus your intelligence on the ultimate source of the opposition that you face; describe your predicament with the greatest possible accuracy. What is the true nature of the conflict? Is it a person or their behavior? Is it a habit, a phrase, or an error of attention? Is this really an attack? Is it intentional? What is being attacked? Is the problem "out there" or "in here"?

Get as close to the core of the issue as possible. Fight the right battle and revise your assessment frequently. Opponents change and alliances shift. If you discover that you have been fighting the wrong battle with the wrong opponent, abandon the effort and readjust.

The deepest root of human fighting behavior is insecurity. Dozens of times each day, each of us asks one basic question of our environment: "Is it safe?" The answer starts a whole cascade of psychological and behavioral responses. If I feel safe, I am inclined to yield, negotiate, reposition, and inquire. If I feel threatened and insecure, I am inclined to take up arms in defense or lash out with an attack.

When confronting resistance, always suspect some underlying insecurity at work—either in yourself, your adversary, or both. If you can create an atmosphere of safety, you can make genuine progress. Threats and unpredictable behavior only increase insecurity and harden resistance. Reduce the insecurity and the resistance will soften.

When he looks for the source of a conflict, the fledgling usually assumes that it lies with the opposing party. He believes that most of the arguments and disagreements in his life are somebody else's fault. Assigning blame is easy; *his* behavior was insensitive, *her* attitude hostile, *their* demands unreasonable. When anger and chaos flare, the fledgling points the finger of blame outward in an attempt to fortify his position and gain a sense of security. Unfortunately, this psychological quick fix usually just makes things worse.

The owl's solution is just the reverse. Instead of resisting further or striking out with accusation, he softens his defensive posture and turns his gaze inward; he turns yin and asks, "Is this conflict the result of my own arrogance, bigotry, or narrow-mindedness? What's my real motivation? What did I do to create this predicament? Could I have acted sooner? What internal adjustments could I make to resolve this situation right now?"

Naturally, we resist this process. When we do look in the mirror, what we see is not always pretty. We see our weaknesses, stupidities, and blind spots. This process may be unpleasant, but it is consistently beneficial. If you do see errors in the mirror, you can adjust. If you don't take the look, you will continue to be a victim of your own myopia.

Introspection offers a double payoff. In the first place, it is contagious and disarming; it creates an atmosphere of safety. To say "It's my fault" in any form deflates an aggressor's hostility. It also adds to self-knowledge, which makes us more effective. Thus the owl looks inward at every opportunity.

Be Active, Not Reactive

> Do not act on first impulse; people will soon recognize
> the uniformity and, by anticipating, frustrate your designs.
> It is easy to kill a bird on the wing that flies straight, not
> so one that twists and turns.
>
> Balthasar Gracian, *The Art of Worldly Wisdom*

> Immature strategy is the cause of grief.
>
> Miyamoto Musashi, *A Book of Five Rings*

The fledgling is a reactor. Every time he experiences a stimulus, his thoughts and behaviors run down the same well-worn course. He lives by links of association, never dreaming that there is a lot more to relationship than cause and effect.

Unfortunately, the fledgling's reactivity makes him predictable, weak, and ineffective. By reacting to his predicament, he is the one who is controlled—he is a victim, not an artist. Worst of all, his behavior does not change to suit evolving conditions. He is stuck.

Reactivity intensifies conflict and builds resistance. When two highly reactive parties come into opposition, the spiral of conflict tightens as each responds reflexively to the aggression of the other. Conflict inspires reaction, which sparks counterreaction, which leads to counter-counterreaction, and eventually to violence that injures both parties.

Historians say that the inferior general is always fighting the last war. He learns one lesson and then reactively applies it to every situation he faces, forgetting that every fight and every enemy is unique. The owl, on the other hand, looks at each conflict with the fresh eyes of seasoned innocence. She learns from the past, but doesn't give it more significance than it deserves. History may repeat itself, but then again, it may fly off in a nonlinear, chaotic leap. Do not be a slave to a historical model. Fight today's fight today.

When we search for effective action, our first response is sometimes the most inspired, meaningful, and appropriate. Sometimes, however, our first reaction is impulsive, foolish, and reactionary. The difference lies in training. The first efforts of a novice pianist are mere noise, but the improvisations of a musical master are spontaneously perfect. The second and third attempts of the novice are likely to be more musical, just as the second and third attempts of a master can be overwrought. The fledgling cannot afford to act on impulse because he has no foundation. The owl can afford this luxury because it springs from disciplined practice.

Ultimately, the owlish objective is to inject some reflection, creativity, and intelligence between stimulus and response. Observe your reactivity as a witness. Do you respond the same way every time someone threatens your territory or disagrees with your position? Is your behavior predictable?

The key to transcending reactivity is awareness. Question both stimulus and response. View the conflict in a wider context. Slow down, breathe, and delay your gratification—do not attempt to satisfy every impulse. Time and patience are great warriors that will keep you out of reactive ruts.

Break up patterns with fresh movement. Choose which fights to fight and which to abandon. If you find yourself locked in a cycle of reactivity, step laterally and innovate your way out. Be unpredictable, even to yourself.

Be a Good Enemy

You may have enemies whom you hate, but not enemies whom you despise. You must be proud of your enemy: then the success of your enemy shall be your success too.

Friedrich Nietzsche, *Thus Spoke Zarathustra*

I choose my friends for their good looks, my acquaintances for their good characters, and my enemies for their intellects. A man cannot be too careful in the choice of his enemies.

Oscar Wilde

Like it or not, you will face resistance and opposition in your life, your profession, and your relationships. There is no escape from this predicament. You could choose to resist, but that would only lead to frustration. The superior approach is to sharpen your skills and increase the quality of your performance. In this, the owl aspires to become an excellent fighter and a good enemy.

The fledgling finds this idea incomprehensible. He makes no distinction between a good enemy and a poor one. He simply wants to be left alone—antagonists get in his way and interfere with his happiness. For the fledgling, the only good enemy is no enemy.

In fact, a good enemy is a creature of immense value. He holds our feet to the fire and makes us dig for new capabilities and latent talents; he makes us stretch. He watches what we pay attention to, and when we become distracted, he reminds us with a clean and focused strike. He challenges us where we are weak, keeps us slightly off balance, and forces us continually to readjust. His tactics are mixed and unpredictable. In this, the good enemy is an ally, a teacher, and possibly even a healer.

The good enemy is sincere. He honors the process of intelligent opposition, respects his opponent, and always preserves face. There is no intent to humiliate in this encounter, only to train for greater excellence in a mutually beneficial process. A good enemy is a rare and wonderful discovery.

The poor enemy, on the other hand, is dull and insensitive. In his ignorance, he attacks strength and weakness indiscriminately. His attacks are neither graceful nor instructive; they are merely violent. His resistance does not regulate or create, it simply generates friction and wears us down. There is little to be gained by engaging a poor enemy, and the owl avoids this whenever possible.

The world is filled with poor enemies. We meet them constantly, people who oppose us at random, lashing out impulsively with words and fists. The owlish way to deal with these poor enemies is to help them improve their performance. Engage them in education combat. Be a good enemy to a poor one. Show him his weaknesses with precise, focused strikes. Honor his skills but strike his vulnerabilities. Expand his comfort zone by keeping him slightly off balance.

Over time, your poor enemy will find new skills. His performance will become more sophisticated and may even surpass your own. But this is a victory, not a defeat. You will have turned a nuisance into an ally, an annoyance into a teacher. There is no way to lose in this effort. At the least, you will defend yourself skillfully and gracefully. If you are adept, you will transform your opponent from a surly, ill-tempered beast into a collaborator in your own pursuit of excellence.

Preempt

Meet the first beginnings; look to the budding mischief before it has time to ripen to maturity.

Shakespeare

He who excels at resolving difficulties does so before they arise. He who excels in conquering his enemies triumphs before threats materialize.

Sun Tzu

The owl sees a fight in her future. Someone is going to abuse her, insult her integrity, or take a swing at her head. Instead of passively waiting for the fateful moment, however, she takes action: She preempts.

Preemption is an extremely economical strategy for managing conflict. When conflict is young, it is malleable. The attacker is not yet consumed by emotion, nor is he fixated on a particular outcome. There are tactical alternatives to choose from, and the risk is low. Since she feels little ambiguity, fear, or time pressure, the owl can stay relaxed and alert. At this point, the art is easy. Small touches can easily quell resistance and nudge a relationship back into alignment.

In her fear and ignorance, the fledgling delays action. But problems deferred tend to grow; procrastination only intensifies her difficulties. The fledgling thinks she's saving effort; but she's actually creating a deeper predicament with each passing moment. As her relationships become increasingly polarized, she will need to wield extremely high levels of skill, energy, and power just to break even. Eventually, all the conflict artistry in the world might not be enough to prevent a violent confrontation.

Thus the owl's objective is to act as early as possible, before resistance materializes. Lao Tzu was the original advocate of preemption:

It is easy to maintain a situation while it is still secure;
It is easy to deal with a situation before symptoms develop;
It is easy to break a thing when it is yet brittle;
It is easy to dissolve a thing when it is yet minute.
Deal with a thing while it is still nothing;
Keep a thing in order before disorder sets in.

This art is subtle; it consists of making small corrections, tiny adjustments, and light touches. It demands keen attention to the smallest details of the evolving dynamic. Put your mind ahead of events. Study the trends and look for the embryonic. As Lao Tzu would have put it, "The owl must work on what is not yet there."

In following the logic of preemptive action, the owl finds that there is no limit to how early she can act. This perspective provides her with a vast number of options and alternatives. The first choice is creative and ecological relationship building. Communication diminishes resistance and softens the violent spirit. These efforts benefit all parties and reduce the likelihood of aggression.

The fledgling does not think of benevolence and respect as self-defense tactics, but these are true martial arts. A creature who is healthy, secure, and content is unlikely to war on her neighbors. Humanitarian efforts are not only the right thing to do, they are the smart thing to do.

When acting preemptively, the level of last resort is destructive force. In this case, the objective is to incapacitate or destroy an opponent before he attacks. This may be necessary in exceptional cases, but for the owl, preemptive strikes constitute a failure of preemptive artistry. If you are preemptively aware, connected, and active, there will be no need to strike. If a time comes to attack preemptively, you are already far too late.

The fledgling sees preemptive action as a tactic for occasional use, but the owl is *always* acting preemptively. Build a network of healthy relationships and transform situations now, before they become conflicted. Fight the fires of the unexpected as you must, but keep your preemptive mind active.

To be idle during times of tranquility is an error; this is precisely the time for vigorous preemptive effort. Create the future in the present. Fight the little fight today so you won't have to fight the big one tomorrow. Exercise a light touch now, and you won't have to deal a lethal blow later. Move early and constructively. You will discover that you rarely, if ever, need to engage an opponent in battle.

Set Limits

To stay alive you have to be able to hold out against equilibrium, maintain imbalance, bank against entropy, and you can only transact this business with membranes.

Lewis Thomas, *Lives of a Cell*

The fledgling has little awareness of boundaries. He does not know the extent of his power and is wildly inconsistent in defending his territory. On some occasions he sets arbitrary boundaries; other times, none at all.

In fact, limits are vital for personal survival and social ecology. In a world of constant flux, it is essential that individuals maintain internal cohesion and order; without boundaries, there could be no life. Thus the owl is keenly aware of his territory. He knows where the boundaries are, who will be allowed to enter, and what he will do if his niche is violated.

When he does set boundaries, the fledgling thinks exclusively in terms of black and white, but the owlish warrior takes inspiration from the intelligence of natural systems. Look at your territory as if it were a single cell. The cell is bounded by a highly selective membrane that allows some substances to pass through, but not others. A healthy cellular membrane is flexible, resilient, and discriminating.

A semipermeable boundary can be hard or soft, depending on needs and temperament. Here the owl makes a conscious choice, establishing hard boundaries in some areas, soft boundaries in others. With a soft line, the owl gives the approaching party the benefit of the doubt. When he draws a hard line, however, he casts the situation rigidly in black-and-white terms. *Either* a person has exceeded the limit *or* he has not. If he has exceeded the limit, he is subject to enforcement. There will be no vacillating and no hesitation, simply swift and decisive action.

The art begins with self-knowledge. The owl clarifies his priorities and values and updates this understanding regularly. He knows the difference between the essential and the optional. He keeps his vital concerns at the center of his attention, where they form a nucleus protected by a strong and resilient boundary. At the same time, he allows his superficial interests to float at the periphery where there is some flexibility in limits and enforcement.

When enforcing a hard line, you may choose to execute a block. This is a focused, highly assertive rejection of the attack that says, "I will not accept this behavior." Focus your words, gestures, and behaviors with clear, assertive intent, just as you would block a punch with a stick or a rigid forearm. Limit the movement with force and power. Well-executed blocks not only preserve integrity, they also send a clear and unambiguous message to the opponent as to where we draw the line.

Some cases are universal. No one has the right to violate our bodies by assault or rape; this requires a hard, black-and-white limit; the attacker has *either* crossed the line, *or* he hasn't. Other areas are best defined with soft, semipermeable boundaries. These are realms where it is more difficult to get precise definition. In these places, the territory to be protected is elusive and subject to interpretation. Here, we must exercise discretion and judgment.

Match your resistance to the intensity and quality of the challenge. Meet bold challenges with assertive action or intelligent weakness. Meet soft challenges with gentle redirection and persuasion. Maintain the integrity of your membrane with a diversity of technique.

Exercise judgment based on context. Some boundaries are permanent and remain in effect under all conditions: A knife to the throat is always an invasion of personal territory. Other boundaries are situational: Some people are allowed to touch our bodies, but only under certain circumstances.

Make it a general practice to communicate your limits clearly to those around you, especially if there is any doubt. The fledgling assumes that others know just how far they can go, but this is an error. Every creature and every culture has a different sense of territory. What is acceptable for one person may be an outrageous imposition for others. Preempt confusion and conflict by educating others about where your personal and organizational limits lie and how rigid they are. Set the boundary with explicit words and gestures. Make yourself clear.

Play the Yin and the Yang

All explicit opposites are implicit allies.

Alan Watts

Combine in yourself the dove and the serpent,
not as a monster but as a prodigy.

Balthasar Gracian, *The Art of Worldly Wisdom*

Imagine that you are standing on one side of a door that is hinged to
swing in both directions. On the other side of the door is an "opponent" who will try to attack you and upset your balance.

You and your opponent can make two basic movements. A push
on the door is a yang movement; it is active and direct. A pull or yield
is a yin movement; it is receptive. The way the relationship develops
depends on the interplay of these yin and yang forces.

Yin and yang may be symmetrical or complementary. Suppose that
your "opponent" decides to "attack" by pushing on the door. If you
meet this push with a push of your own, you make a symmetrical response. In symmetry, yang meets yang or yin meets yin. Arm wrestling
is a symmetrical relationship; push meets push. "Tug of war" is also
symmetrical; pull meets pull.

The symmetrical relationship is simple. You push me, I push you
back. You make wild accusations about my behavior, I make wild accusations about your behavior. You threaten me, I threaten you. Tit for
tat, eye for eye, tooth for tooth. This is the logic of symmetry. Each act
of aggression is countered with an attempt to even the score.

In a purely symmetrical relationship, strength is useful, at least in
the short term. If you can push harder on the door than I can, you will

"win." Your victory is likely to be short-lived, however, because I will try to even the score. I will get up off the floor and push back with all the strength I can muster. I will call for vengeance and claim "an eye for an eye."

In cybernetic terms, symmetry is a prescription for disaster. Push-for-push sets off a cycle of positive feedback in which each act of aggression creates more aggression in return. If both parties are intent on responding symmetrically, escalation and violence are virtually inevitable.

In this relationship, everyone suffers. Gandhi recognized this clearly: "To punish and destroy an oppressor is merely to initiate a new cycle of violence and oppression." In the owl's quest for ecological human relationships, symmetry is usually a dead end. As the saying goes, "An eye for an eye and a tooth for a tooth soon leads to an eyeless and toothless world."

Even as a self-defense strategy, symmetry has significant drawbacks. The fledgling assumes that the stronger his push, the better the result, so he attacks the door with a mighty burst of power. But here the extreme leads to its opposite. If his opponent withdraws his opposition, the fledgling's strength and momentum will carry him crashing to the floor. Here, power actually becomes a liability. This is what the ancients called "the weakness of strength."

The pattern is familiar. The more aroused we get, the harder we push. Eventually, symmetry takes on a life of its own and we begin to push harder than we ever intended. Our thoughts and behavior get more and more out of control as the conflict intensifies. Later, we realize how far out of balance we were, but by then it is too late. Symmetry has done its damage. We have been thrown by our own power.

Symmetrical strategies are primitive, but they are not without value and they do have a place in the owl's repertoire. They are useful for setting limits and are sometimes essential for survival. If the owl is cornered, he may have no choice but to strike back. In some cases, symmetry can even prevent conflict from starting in the first place. When the bully pushes the door and meets resistance, he may simply give up and go away. As Shivas Irons, the shamanic golf pro in Michael Murphy's *Golf in the Kingdom,* put it, "Sometimes ther's nae better way to kill a dragon than to charge right up to it and shove a spear down its throat."

Some believe that symmetrical conflict behaviors are inherently evil, but this is not the case. The real problem is in the shallowness of our repertoires—many of us know of no other way to relate. No matter what the person on the other side of the door does, we resist symmetrically. This is a particularly vicious form of tunnel vision.

The alternative approach is the complementary response: the yielding, nonresistant behavior. If the door is pulled, the owl pushes; if the door is pushed, she pulls. She meets yang with yin, force with softness. Complementary movements are paradoxical and counterintuitive; they are the opposite of what an attacker is likely to expect.

When crafting a complementary behavior, strength is not particularly important. The essential skills are sensitivity, timing, and flexibility. Here the conflict artist guides the attacker's motion and uses it to immobilize or throw him.

In hand-to-hand combat, complementary movements are highly effective. The secret lies in your ability to harness the motion inherent in the aggressor's attack. Sense the motion and yield in synchrony with the thrust of the strike. Wield your weakness intelligently. If your timing is right, the aggressor will lose his balance and fall.

This practice is called "the art of fighting without fighting." It is also called "using the attacker's energy against him." The symmetrical fighter expects to encounter resistance, so he summons up a great burst of energy and pushes as strongly as possible. When the resistance disappears, he loses his balance and falls. This illustrates the "strength of weakness."

Lao Tzu was the original master of this art:

What you want to compress you must first truly allow to expand.
What you want to weaken you must first allow to grow strong.
What you want to destroy you must first allow to truly flourish.
From whoever you want to take away, you must first truly give.
This is called being clear about the invisible.
The soft wins victory over the hard. The weak wins victory over the strong.

Complementary responses take advantage of the natural limitations inherent in most forms of attack. The attacker's punch has a natural range of effectiveness, a power stroke that is limited by body mechanics. If his fist is very close to his body or highly extended away from his body, his attack will be weak and ineffective. All forms of attack have similar characteristics; they are weak, then strong, then weak.

We see this clearly in military battles over territory. When one country attacks another, there is a certain optimal distance for best effectiveness. An armed force depends on supply lines to keep it stocked with food, fuel, and ammunition. If the front line becomes extended too far from the center, supply lines become weak and soldiers run short. At this point, they are extremely vulnerable.

Observe these natural limitations in your practice. When defending, do not engage an attack in the midst of its natural power stroke. Instead, act selectively; move early or late. Nip the problem in the bud or get out of the way to act later as the power of the attack begins to fade. By being nonresistant at the right time, you can lead, control, reverse, or defeat the attack as necessary.

No matter what tactical choice you make in a conflict, commit strongly to your chosen course of action. Push or yield with conviction. Do not attempt to defend yourself with tentative and incomplete movements. Make bold strokes. You are safer with a committed movement or action than with any half measure.

At the same time, recognize the dangers of extending beyond your natural range or motion or influence. Headlong rushes are just as dangerous as tentative, half-hearted movements. Any extension beyond your natural range will compromise your balance and put you at risk. If you approach the limits of your strength, exercise increasing caution. Act fully and completely.

When crafting a complementary response to an attack, it is essential to give the attack someplace to go. Allow the attack to express itself and run its natural course. Shape the aggression as you must, but interfere as little as possible. Get out of the way and create a void for the attacker to fall into. There is risk here to be sure, but sensitivity and mobility can keep you safe.

Follow this path in conversation. Give your opponent's argument someplace to go by acknowledging it, especially if you disagree. Instead of countering his outrageous arguments, give them some credit. Illuminate your adversary's path with acceptance, inquiry, and even encouragement. This will disarm him, leaving him slack-jawed and flat-footed, wondering what happened to the resistance that he expected. If he foolishly elects to pursue his course even further, he will simply accelerate his own downfall.

At the highest skill level, the complementary response is perfectly counterintuitive. Not only does the owl yield, he actually amplifies the power of his opponent's attack. He cooperates with enthusiastic agreement; he assists the attacker in his efforts to strike. At this point, attacker and defender are perfectly synchronized. The additional energy of cooperation helps the attacker go far beyond his normal state of balance and sends him crashing to the ground.

Complementary responses are effective, but they are not infallible. If you are too yielding, or if your timing is off, you will get smashed by the door. A poorly executed yin response can lead to disaster. Therefore, the owl does not yield indiscriminately at the door; he executes with sensitivity and awareness. Do not go limp! The complementary response is an assertive form of selective and intelligent yielding; it is never passive. If you choose to turn your cheek to complement an attack, do it intelligently, actively, and creatively. Maintain your balance, center, and integrity at all times

Complementary responses demand a high level of physical, intellectual, and spiritual flexibility. There must be some give in your physical, psychic, and social posture. Yielding at the door implies the ability to change position—to change your mind.

A high level of self-knowledge is essential. The aspiring owl must know how far he can yield and how hard he can push. How much can you give up without compromising your integrity? How much force can you bring to bear? What are the limits to your strength? Develop this knowledge through exposure and experience.

In the end, complementary responses are the key to creativity. The process works best in cyclic combination with symmetry. The artist struggles long and hard against the metaphorical door, only to experience a sudden rush of insight as he relaxes his effort. This suggests that our creative endeavors should be rhythmic oscillations of hard and soft, pushing and yielding. The hard push on the door is logical, purposive, and intentional striving toward an objective; it is conscious work. The yield on the door is the release of intuition. By alternating these yin and yang strategies, you will nurture your creativity.

Executing a single yang or yin response is easy. Even the fledgling can recognize the difference between an active push and a yielding pull. The more sophisticated art is to master the improvisational transitions from yin to yang and yang to yin. Since conditions and opponents are always changing, this dynamic dexterity is the most essential of all skills. Neither mode is good in itself; what is good is the ability to move gracefully from one to the other.

Observe the myriad creatures. The dog can go from a growling, territorial beast to a playful puppy in an instant. Children can be blood enemies one moment and best friends the next. Their transition from yang to yin and yin to yang is effortless.

Neither yin nor yang is good in itself. Only in dynamic combination can they be truly effective. Strive for a unity of expression. Seek a comprehensive style that honors both potentials simultaneously. Stay centered in the midst of yin and yang. Hold both together in a dynamic unity. Be disposed to neither, but be capable of both. Fly with both wings.

See the Illusion

The greatest cunning is to have none at all.

Carl Sandburg

As a warrior in constant pursuit of the truth, the owl is well versed in the ways of illusion and guile. She understands the ways in which perception can be distorted and manipulated by clever opponents. This knowledge serves her in two ways: She can protect herself from duplicity and, if necessary, she can wield it skillfully to preserve her integrity.

The art of deception consists of two basic methods: hiding the real and showing the false. Hiding the real is a tactic of concealment; here the objective is to prevent the opponent from learning the true extent of our capabilities. The sly deceiver might use carefully crafted words and phrases to conceal her power or intentions. She might shroud herself in mystery, use camouflage, or have a concealed weapon. This is a versatile and effective technique.

Showing the false is the complementary approach. There are two ways to do this: You may show false strength, or you may show false weakness.

In the animal world, cats and dogs show false strength by raising the hair on their necks and backs. Birds extend their wings and ruffle their feathers to appear larger than life. In the human world, people show false strength with exaggerated posture and overblown words.

Showing false strength is a form of deterrence and bluff. Though popular, this strategy has serious flaws. In the first place, it hinges on the opponent's rationality; the deceiver is betting that a sensible opponent will avoid the possibility of powerful retaliation and withhold his attack. This is a gamble, however, because there is no way to tell how a person might respond. Showing false strength might actually trigger the attack that you were trying to prevent in the first place; some opponents actually prefer to attack strength.

Showing false weakness is the complementary approach. Here the deceiver tries to be perceived as less capable than she actually is. Sun Tzu was a strong advocate of this method: "Pretend inferiority and encourage his arrogance." This is the mythic tactic of the wise old tai ch'i master. His posture and demeanor makes it appear as though he is crippled and slow, but this is a ruse. In fact, he is agile and powerful.

Showing false weakness is a highly sophisticated tactic that reveals insight into the combative personality. Many aggressors are not interested in fighting the weak. If there is no challenge, there is no motivation to fight. The wisdom of this understanding explains why the old tai ch'i master is, in fact, so old.

The deceiver can also use false weakness as bait to lure an opponent. This is the tactic used by birds that fake a broken wing to lure intruders away from the nest. If you intentionally show a weakness or opening, you will know with high probability what action your opponent will take. This gives you a tremendous advantage.

Or you may "bait and switch." Present an advantage and then withdraw it, replacing it with something less friendly. Sun Tzu: "Offer the enemy a bait to lure him; feign disorder and strike him." This maneuver is effective, but it also instructs us to be extremely careful when taking advantage of apparent weakness: You may be walking into a trap. As Sun Tzu warns, "Do not gobble proffered baits." If the offer or opening appears enticing, be wary. Maintain a sense of center and do not go to extremes. Strike the weakness as necessary, but do not overcommit. If an opening or opportunity seems too good to be true, it probably is.

Of all the variations on false weakness, playing dumb is by far the most fascinating. Superficially, this is a stealth tactic that allows the deceiver to operate in disguise and assess a situation from the inside. It is fundamental for all sorts of covert operations. But playing dumb is also a special case, a scheme that is not a scheme. The dumb "act" succeeds as deception, but it also succeeds because it is far closer to the truth of our existence as fallible human beings. Here the wise deceiver finds a flawless strategy. It counters our tendency to overestimate our knowledge and skills, while simultaneously disarming our adversaries or luring them into overextension. In this, playing dumb is a no-lose ruse.

To the fledgling, deceptive tactics appear to be highly economical. A small amount of energy invested in duplicity can generate a large payoff in safety or tactical advantage. But as a truly useful and long-term path, deception has limited use.

Deception can fail in a number of ways—some local, others systemic. Remember that deceptive practices affect *both* parties. When you create a ruse, your attention becomes fragmented and you can no longer focus on a single objective. Not only does the liar need a good memory, he also needs focused attention: Maintaining a lie, which often becomes a series of lies, easily becomes debilitating and consuming.

Deception always increases stress. You think: "My opponent expects me to strike high, so I will strike low. He expects me to move right, so I will move left." This is fine as far as it goes, but the process doesn't stop there. You suspect that your opponent knows your intent, so you calculate double-reverse, triple-reverse, and quadruple-reverse psychologies. You eventually become so distracted by your calculations that you lose sight of your original objective. At this point, an honest opponent may simply step in and knock you to the ground.

To make things worse, deception also pollutes social ecosystems. If you deceive me, I feel justified in deceiving you. You will then respond with more duplicity and cunning. At this point, even the most sincere gestures will be greeted with suspicion. With each new act of duplicity, it becomes more difficult to deal with each other. In this way, fraud can be just as destructive as force. Keep this in mind when choosing tactics, and use deception with the same degree of restraint that you would force. Save it for when you really need it.

On the surface, deception appears to be simple: Put up a false front, distort a few facts, stretch a story, and capitalize on your advantage. But in fact, these are not beginner's tactics. Hiding the real and showing the false require high levels of sustained concentration, and the risks are great. If you choose deception, do it from a foundation of solid training and self-knowledge. Build proficiency in the fundamentals first; concentrate your attention on your own natural capabilities and the basic skills of your discipline. Then, if necessary, manipulate perceived reality. As Sun Tzu put it, "Apparent confusion is a product of good order; apparent cowardice, of courage; apparent weakness, of strength."

In the vast majority of cases, honesty is the owl's policy of choice. Reserve a place in your repertoire for deception, but use it sparingly. Lay a false trail when necessary, but always with caution, awareness, and restraint. As Balthasar Gracian put it in *The Art of Worldly Wisdom,* "Use, but do not abuse cunning. One ought not to delight in it, still less to boast of it."

Conserve Face

The gentleman calls attention to the good points
in others; he does not call attention to their defects.
The small man does just the reverse of this.

Confucius, *The Analects*

The fledgling talks trash. He mocks and ridicules his opponents, attempting to intimidate them with verbal jabs and abuse. He believes that by putting his adversaries down, his stature is thereby increased.

The owl rejects these tactics. He treats opponents as well as allies with sincere respect. This is not simply a matter of courtesy; it is a matter of pragmatic intelligence. Human beings and organizations are fundamentally unpredictable. Appearances deceive; an opponent may be far more capable than he appears. An adversary may acquire new knowledge, new allies, or new capabilities. Recognizing this, the owl acknowledges his opponent's potential, for excellence as well as for treachery.

In all cases, treat your opponent as an equal and never take an encounter lightly. Never assume that victory will be easy or that you are totally safe. Never assume that your position is secure. There is always someone who is bigger, stronger, faster, smarter, or luckier. By paying respect, you keep your mind open and alert.

One of the worst tactical errors you can make in a conflicted relationship is to take away an opponent's "face." Face is the reflection we see in our fellows' eyes; it is our standing in community. As social creatures, we value this reflection immensely. The acknowledgment and acceptance of our families, friends, and colleagues are of pivotal importance. To lose face is to diminish our very identity.

There is nothing to be gained by taking away an opponent's face; this is a victory without substance. When you take away an opponent's face, he is likely to become uncooperative, angry, unpredictable or violent. Loss of face means exposure and vulnerability. Position and reputation are no longer secure. Escalation and retaliation are likely.

From a tactical perspective, taking away face will get you nowhere. When you put someone down, your position is in no way improved. All it does is pollute the web of relationship. When you ridicule another, you lose.

Knowing this, the owl always preserves face. He may hit an opponent, sue him, or have him arrested, but will always allow him to maintain his personal dignity. Do not destroy a reputation unless it is unavoidable.

The positive side of this art is actively to give face to an opponent. Build up her self-image and status, even if you despise her. Acknowledge her position, value, and dignity. Feed her sense of self-worth. These gestures cost little but pay greatly. Active gifts of face will make her more compliant and receptive, and, captivated by her own sense of greatness, she may even overcommit and throw herself.

Sadly, the fledgling believes that respect for an adversary is a sign of weakness. He believes that a warrior should be supremely confident of victory at all times, and that acknowledging an opponent's power, skill, or intelligence is the attitude of a loser. The owl, on the other hand, makes no claims to invulnerability and is quick to point out his opponent's potential for high performance or, at the very least, for a lucky break.

In the owl's eyes, respect is a sign of intelligence and a no-lose proposition. When you practice this art, you acknowledge your opponent's capacity for skill, adaptability, learning, and intelligence. This is a pragmatic and intelligent approach to fighting, but it also sets the stage for creative resolution. When your opponent feels that he is being taken seriously, he will soften his resistance and approach the middle ground. Position yourself for the future. Alliances shift; today's opponent may be tomorrow's ally. Respect keeps the door open.

Synchronize

When the strike of a hawk breaks the body of
its prey, it is because of timing.

Sun Tzu, *The Art of War*

Ripeness is all.

Shakespeare

In hand-to-hand combat, good timing is clearly essential. The defender who acts too early or late may be injured or killed. The good fighter is one who can sense his opponent's movement and synchronize his strikes to fill the gaps.

For the owl, however, the idea of being "on time" applies to every dimension of conflicted relationship. At all levels, temporal synchrony makes the difference between mediocre performance and art. That which inflames and escalates in one moment may calm and soothe in the next. Positive feedback today might be negative feedback tomorrow. The same word, gesture, or expression can be a spectacular success or a devastating failure, depending on when we execute. An early hard-style response can mean unnecessary escalation and even destruction; a late soft-style response can lead to a humiliating defeat.

The fledgling believes that being on time is a trivial concern and so neglects this art. The owl, on the other hand, knows that timeliness saves wasted effort and makes his efforts more effective. An action that is executed on time requires far less force than one that comes early or late. Whenever we are off time, we waste energy, create tension, reduce effectiveness, and make ourselves vulnerable. Thus the owl becomes his own ally; he hones his timing skills at all levels.

Temporal precision begins with sensitivity and awareness. Extend your intelligence into your environment and make yourself familiar with the history of your predicament. What is the background? What are the trends? How does the resistance change over time? Is this a static deadlock, an escalation, or a pattern of weakening resistance? Survey conditions and make tentative predictions. Then listen to the deep body. Hear the faint whispers that tell of expanding and contracting temporal margins.

The fledgling believes that he must always be in a hurry in order to be on time, but this is not the case. The objective is to match pace with the context of experience. If events are moving slowly, your pace should also be slow. If things are moving quickly, you must accelerate. Of course, the pace of events is always changing, so you must regulate your movement accordingly. Seek a perfect correspondence. Intercept the target in flight.

The owl excels at temporal performance because he accepts an optimal level of challenges. He leaves generous time margins for all tasks and a little extra for the unexpected. This improves his performance dramatically; he is more relaxed, balanced, and effective in all phases of his life. He has the psychic space to pay attention.

Naturally, the most owlish approach is to establish temporal synchrony at the very beginning of each task and maintain it continuously. In spite of our best efforts, however, we sometimes get behind the action and experience time trouble. As temporal margins shrink, skills decay and our attention fragments. Mind–body unity begins to disintegrate, and we find it difficult to think globally or objectively. When time trouble becomes severe, we see only the most striking elements of the situation and lurch desperately toward the superficially obvious solutions. We lose sight of our objectives as we juggle the demands of the immediate crisis. Instead of acting creatively, we begin to react desperately.

If you find yourself in time trouble, acknowledge it immediately. Redouble your concentration and give up the search for an ideal solution. Usually, several reasonable options are available. Take one of them; decisive action will bring you back into temporal alignment. If you can step outside the flow of events without compromising your position or objectives, do so. Ignore the extraneous and concentrate on the basics. Be prepared for this ahead of time. Know the difference between the disposable and the essential.

Synchrony is not the only timing skill, of course. The aspiring owl must also know how to break timing. You can use this tactic on a number of levels. Syncopate your personal rhythms to break out of reactive ruts and keep yourself slightly off balance. Shift the accent to the half-beat to motivate yourself in new directions. Play with the edges of predictability to disrupt your opponent's timing and gain advantage. Establish rhythms, break them into new patterns, and then reestablish. Naturally, this is an advanced practice that springs from mastery of the fundamentals.

Refine your temporal precision by working from the coarse to the fine, from the macro to the micro. Once you have integrated a base level of temporal precision into your activity, work toward more subtle timings. Power the effort with commitment. Walk your talk. If you give your word to be there at dawn, be there.

Temporal precision builds on itself. The more often you are on time, the more intimacy you will develop with other creatures and your environment. The more connected you are, the more precise your temporal performance will be. Each contributes to the other. Eventually, there will be no gap between perception and right action. Integration leads to synchrony.

Have No Doubt

When the blast of war blows in our ears,
Then imitate the action of the tiger;
Stiffen the sinews, summon up the blood,
Disguise fair nature with hard-favour'd rage.

Shakespeare

In death ground, fight.

Sun Tzu

Even as she becomes highly proficient at maneuver and strategy, the owl may still have the misfortune to be violently attacked by strong and hostile aggressors. These encounters are rare events, but we must give the possibility due consideration. After all, we are vulnerable creatures in a sometimes violent world. We can do everything right—extend awareness, avoid dangerous places, build healthy relationships—and still be violently attacked.

The first step in surviving a worst-case situation is recognition. Unfortunately, there is no model for this experience and no two situations are identical. A worst-case encounter may develop slowly over hours, days, or weeks, or it may strike spontaneously and without warning. In all cases, look for a direct and immediate threat to survival. In a true worst-case situation, failure to defend will lead to catastrophe.

If you are forced into a worse-case situation, integrate all your energies into a single, furious effort. Focus totally on staying alive. Abandon your fear by channeling it into anger and action. Put every tissue fiber into the here and now. Allow no cell to tend to anything other than the immediate demands of the present. Go for the trachea, the jugular vein, or the knees with the full force of your animal body and spirit.

In a worst-case encounter, mental state is *the* determining factor. No amount of skill or technique can make up for a lack of intensity or a failure to assert the right to self-defense. Thus the owl assumes a state of zero doubt; she acts with complete certainty and conviction. This certainty transcends limitations in skill and guarantees a powerful response.

The zero-doubt state is dead serious, in-your-face ego-logic. It is a willingness to engage the enemy, a total abandonment to the fight. There is no gray area here. It is perfect black-and-white commitment.

Animals are the ultimate masters of this zero-doubt art. Since they live on the cutting edge of survival, they know zero-doubt intimately and can tap into it without hesitation. Observe the wild creatures and imagine the naked reality of their ultimate encounters. Take that intensity into your body and make it your own.

Develop your ability to access this state of complete conviction now, before the ultimate moment actually occurs. Think about your right to defend your life. Does anyone have the right to violate your body? Do you have a natural birthright to self-preservation? Ask the hard questions about what you are willing to do in a crisis. Unless you establish some prior conviction, there is little chance that you will be able to access the zero-doubt state when crisis seizes you by the throat.

Exercise the zero-doubt art when necessary, but do not attempt to exercise it as a full-time mental style. Zero doubt is a short-term solution that, if used beyond immediate crisis, easily reverts to overextension and self-defeat. Zero doubt means zero revision and thus zero learning. When used compulsively in the long term, zero-doubt attitudes stunt growth and produce rigid, dogmatic bullies. Apply the zero-doubt mindset with discretion and reserve it for cases that are truly exceptional. Harness the power when you must, then let it go.

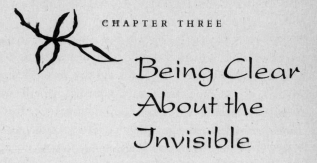

CHAPTER THREE

Being Clear About the Invisible

Inquire

Ignorance is the womb of monsters.

Henry Ward Beecher

When faced with resistance, the fledgling acts first, talks first, pushes first, or retreats first. After the smoke clears, he wonders what happened and why he ended up in such a predicament; he makes his inquiry after the fact. Even worse, he sometimes acts first and ask *no* questions later. Clearly, the fledgling has it backwards.

Every owl knows that knowledge equals options and options equal power. Questions are the basic tools for expanding intelligence and sparking creativity. Not only is the unexamined life not worth living, the unexamined fight is not worth fighting, the unexamined discipline is not worth practicing, and the unexamined strategy is not worth pursuing.

Lead with inquiry. Put your curiosity and intelligence ahead of your behavior. Question all levels of your experience, from the most global and philosophical to the most detailed and specific. Question your environment, your culture, your objectives, your motivations, your training, and your teachers. Question any ideology or doctrine that encourages extremes of conflict behavior. Question any philosophy that discourages the exercise of personal judgment and intelligence. Position yourself on the cutting edge of understanding. Ask questions first, then talk, move, yell, strike, or retreat as necessary.

Extend vision and intelligence into the future by asking "What if" questions. By considering a range of possibilities before they happen, you will stand a much better chance of acting appropriately. "What if" questions force us to acknowledge situations that lie outside our normal experience, and they will often make the difference between in-spired action and awkward reaction. For the fledgling who fails to ask these questions, meeting the future is like flying into a dark and dangerous sky. All he can do is to react to the next challenge when it comes along. But the owl who asks "What if" begins to see in the dark.

The first rule of inquiry is that you can't ask a good question if you think that you already know the answer. Thus, in order to make a truly creative inquiry, you must abandon assumptions and preconceptions. Strip away everything that you believe is useful and relevant and stand in the midst of your ignorance. Be willing to get lost. If necessary, improvise your own disciplines. Dare to be naive and analyze the obvious. There is value in incompetence. Not knowing is the beginning of knowing.

Reflect

If you know the enemy and know yourself, you need
not fear the result of a hundred battles. If you know yourself but not the enemy, for every victory gained you will
also suffer a defeat. If you know neither the enemy nor
yourself, you will succumb in every battle.

Sun Tzu

Above the temple of Apollo at Delphi, the ancient Greeks inscribed
the motto "Know thyself." This is the fundamental principle for anyone who wants to stay alive, resolve a conflict, or defend legitimate interests. It is the sine qua non of owlhood, the essential ingredient in all
martial artistry. For the owl, the first priority in conflict and creativity
is to know her own capabilities.

The fledgling, who enters into conflict without self-knowledge, is
extremely vulnerable not only to the whims of opponents, but to her
own confusion and ignorance. Since she has no idea what her powers
are, she cannot hope to perform at a high level.

The owl, on the other hand, knows her skills, weaknesses, values,
and priorities. Since she has contemplated these issues in advance, she
knows what she can give up and what's worth fighting for—she won't
have to make wild guesses when the heat is on. She may not be able to
predict what her adversary will do, but she can avoid major errors. She
works from a position of strength.

Self-knowledge is not bestowed on us; it must be gained through
experience and participation. The key is exposure. Get naked. Strip
away security and position yourself on the cutting edge of learning
and adaptation. Seek out experiences at the boundary of your comfort
zone. Ambiguity and hardship will teach you what you need to know.

The actual activity is almost irrelevant. What is important is your willingness to go to the limit of your ability, to put yourself on the line, physically or psychologically. Act from a place of ignorance and incompetence. Learn from the ground up.

Self-knowledge begins with the realization that we are driven by two contradictory motivations. The first is curiosity. We want to learn more about our bodies, each other, and the universe around us. Thus we open ourselves to the world, its creatures, and its wondrous possibilities. We make ourselves vulnerable.

Our environment is exquisitely rich, however, and holds many forces that are unfriendly and distinctly dangerous. Realizing this, we strive to protect ourselves. We defend and insulate. We limit our exposure.

Faced with contrasting objectives, we live our lives in oscillation, moving back and forth between curiosity and protection, between vulnerability and defensiveness, constantly seeking the perfect balance. The challenge is to apply the right strategy at the right time; but in order to do this, we have to know the difference.

The problem is not defense. Our world is, after all, both friendly and unfriendly. The problem comes with unconscious, reactive, and inappropriate defense. Here the fledgling is in the dark. A large proportion of her energy and lifestyle is devoted to unconscious protection. She selects friends, career, and ideology to build a protective shell around herself. If pressed, she would say that she is open-minded, but she is really blocking and defending. She thinks that she is learning about herself, but she is really hiding behind a wall.

There are fine lines here; an activity that is educational one day may be protective and anti-educational the next. What's defensive for one person may be risk-taking for another. Two people read the same book. For one it is a challenging glimpse into another world, a chance to expand his comfort zone. For the other it is pure defense, a shield to protect his beliefs and confirm his worldview.

Feel the difference in your body. A genuine educational experience is necessarily ambiguous; it is likely to feel insecure, confusing, and threatening. The protective effort, on the other hand, feels safe, comfortable, and familiar. Since it takes place within the boundaries of the comfort zone, there is no challenge and thus no stress.

Knowing this difference, the owl keeps a watchful eye on her behavior and motivations. She recognizes the tendency to lapse into unnecessary self-protection and questions her behaviors: "Is this embrace or protection? Is this a defense masquerading as education and vulnerability?"

The fledgling, of course, is inclined to avoid this pursuit of self-knowledge altogether. After all, looking in the mirror can be disturbing. No one enjoys coming face to face with her weaknesses, stupidities, and blind spots. This misses the point, however. The owl doesn't necessarily like everything she sees, but she makes the effort nonetheless. The point of the process is not to learn to endure pain, but to make our lives richer and more effective. If you do see errors in the mirror, you can adjust, eliminate problems before they surface, and position yourself for advantage. Through introspection, you can modify your behavior to better fit your environment and relationships. The result is less wasted effort, fewer unproductive fights, less anxiety, and better quality of life.

It is far better to know the dragons within than to suffer their effects unconsciously. Once you know your potential for anger or fear or aggression, you can work with it and position yourself to minimize its effects. Once you know your tendency to react, procrastinate, or act symmetrically, you can anticipate it and adjust.

The fledgling dabbles in reflection from time to time, living under the illusion that self-knowledge is a task that can actually be completed. As he gains experience and meets challenges, he gains a sense of self-familiarity and mistakenly accepts this as his final, established personality. The process, however, can never be truly complete. Every individual is deep and fantastically complicated; we contain multitudes. It is not as if you can look in the mirror, recognize yourself, and have it done with. This is a lifetime enterprise. If you come to a point where you think you are finished, you are, in fact, finished.

Embrace the Dragon

Understand him thoroughly, and lead him
to the point where he is without fault.

Chuang Tzu

When the fledgling meets resistance, he either takes up arms in a furious counterattack or runs away at the earliest opportunity. The owl, on the other hand, begins with a study of the resistance that he faces. He asks, "What are my opponent's short- and long-term objectives? Does he have a target in mind, or is he simply aggressing out of instinct or frustration? What are his skills and blind spots?"

To control the enemy, you must know and, to a certain extent, obey his nature. The more you know about your opposition, the more effectively you can blend and redirect. As always, knowledge is power, ignorance is vulnerability.

The working principle is simple: Never take your eyes off the source of resistance. Maintain contact with his ego, situation, and interests. See through his eyes. Imagine his predicament down to its finest detail. Then get inside his skin, feel his emotions, and think his thoughts. Give up your ego, values, and interests, at least for a time. Throw yourself into the opposing role and live that experience. The more you identify with your opponent, the safer you will ultimately be.

When the fledgling creates an image of "other," he errs by projecting his own experience; he assumes that the other party thinks like he thinks, lives like he lives, and values what he values. He universalizes his personality and assumes that others automatically share his beliefs, feelings, and worldview. If the fledgling feels it, thinks it, desires it, or hates it, then the "other" must too.

This is a serious error. All others, whether they be partners or enemies, have their own unique characteristics, habits, worldview, and brain chemistry. Their reactions and values are likely to be different from our own. Recognizing this, the owl never assumes that his adversary shares any of his perspective. He builds up an image of his opponent from scratch.

In order to act creatively, you must know the true nature of the resistance that you face. You must know where your opponent is and what his intentions are. Therefore it is essential that you stay connected. Stick to your opposition and leave no gaps. Embrace the resistance as if your life depended on it. Feel its slightest vibration and change of intent.

The fledgling, of course, does precisely the opposite. Because of his fear and anxiety, he breaks contact. He feels safer, but this is a perilous illusion. As soon as the link is severed, he loses crucial knowledge and becomes vulnerable. A broken connection is a gap in relationship; an opponent may decide to fill it with a harsh word, a fist, a hostile takeover, or a cruise missile. When you break contact, you lose your ability to predict what your adversary will do. When the attack comes, it will seem random or unprovoked, but this is only a failure of your attention.

Staying connected is a highly paradoxical art because it requires that we focus on the very thing that frightens or aggravates us. But this is, in fact, where the safety lies. The party who is more vigilant in the art of connection is the one who will ultimately prevail.

The process is inherently counterintuitive. In your effort to know your partner, you must study him intensively. You must get inside his skin, feel his sensations, think his thoughts, and dream his dreams. In this way, a curious bond develops; you may actually begin to identify with your opponent and his predicament. Here the martial extreme of polarized combat can lead to its opposite. Severe enmity can lead to bonding, even friendship and alliance. Knowledge breeds understanding; understanding breeds empathy.

Acknowledge this possibility, but maintain your watchfulness. At worst, you will be prepared to meet your opponent's assaults. At best, you will prepare the way for a synergistic resolution and shared understanding. Don't be surprised if hostility begins to fade with time. Enmity is often the breeding ground for alliance.

See Through Bird's Eyes

> If you do not look at things on a large scale,
> it will be difficult for you to master strategy.
>
> Miyamoto Musashi, *A Book of Five Rings*

The owl's master perspective is, naturally, the bird's-eye view. This is the comprehensive view that scans the entire panorama of experience from horizon to horizon. Taking this view means grasping the totality of the environment in which a conflict takes place. As author Robert Heinlein would have put it, the owl can "grok" the entire scene.

Because of her superior perspective, the owl can see and appreciate the interests, needs, values, strengths, and weaknesses of herself and her opposition. She can see the context in which the conflict takes place. Her peripheral and long-range vision is outstanding. She can see not only the center, but the surrounding influences and possible outcomes.

The owl's skill lies in her ability to sweep her attention over the behavior and well-being of entire relationships and systems. She evaluates her actions and behavior in terms of what effect they will have on the totality of the larger family, organization, species, and biosphere. Thinking globally is a metaskill, a way of using basic knowledge.

There are many spheres of reference you can attend to. Look beyond the immediate present and the local space. Be broadly curious. Just as a regional war takes place in the larger context of planetary survival, so too does an argument between friends take place within a community. Study the totality of the situation; evaluate your objectives and relationships in terms of a wide frame of reference; see the gestalt. Then practice shifting your perspective. Move from the broad to the narrow and back again. Reframe the conventional wisdom. Look both from the center and from the periphery. Shift with fluidity from one perspective to another.

Global thinking contributes strongly to strategic intelligence; the bird's-eye view will make you a smart and effective fighter. Your broad vision will allow you to see unconventional options that are invisible to the local thinker or specialist.

A global perspective will also serve you by reducing your ego to a smaller proportion of the total picture. The fledgling would prefer to be a big bird in a small sky, but the owl sees the wisdom of the reverse. As his sense of self-importance fades into insignificance, the path to intelligence becomes clear. Humility is essential to the process. The smaller your ego, the greater the scope of your vision and the more penetrating your insight. When ego no longer blocks the view, you will become capable of creative and inspired action. There is strength in smallness.

Test and Relinquish

> I make a point of never having any prejudices and of
> following docilely wherever the facts may lead me.
>
> Sherlock Holmes

Because she deals with challenging and occasionally life-threatening conflicts, the owl places an extremely high value on discovering the truth. She knows that failure to discriminate between fact and fiction will make her vulnerable. Trying to block an imaginary punch or strike an imaginary target will inevitably lead to trouble. At best, illusion and distortion are expensive distractions; at worst, they can kill. If you want to perform with grace and fluidity, you must address things as they truly are.

Thus the owl practices the art of science. This art is specifically designed to strip away illusion, misconception, and fallacious beliefs and penetrate to the core of what is real.

Unfortunately, the fledgling misunderstands this process. He believes that science works by postulating theories about reality and then trying to prove them correct. When he tries to follow this approach in his daily life, he generates a theory—"My neighbor is aggressive and hostile"—and then looks for "evidence" to support it—"He looks suspicious." He then declares his theory "proved."

This is not how science works. Owlish scientists do not just look for evidence to support their theories, nor do they prove their theories correct. Instead, they look for contradictory evidence and revise their theories accordingly. In fact, scientists are actually in the business of *disproving* theories.

The process begins with speculation and conjecture. The scientist generates a hypothesis, then exposes it to the test of reality. In this effort, there is no attempt to prove anything. In fact, progress comes when ideas or parts of ideas are shown to be false. When this happens, erroneous ideas can be modified or rejected. Through continual speculation, testing and revision, the scientist can move closer to the true nature of things.

The key element in this process is our willingness to discard and revise images that are incorrect. Unfortunately, we resist this process. Our images give us a sense of security. If there is a difference between image and reality, we become angry and upset with reality and its failure to conform to the pictures in our mind. This is like drawing a picture of a mountain and then getting mad at the mountain because it looks different from the drawing. This reaction is completely backward. Instead of guarding and defending our images, we should adjust them to correspond to reality.

Unfortunately, the fledgling believes that changing one's mind is an act of weakness. She believes in consistency and strength of character. But this belief ultimately subverts her intelligence. Intellectual and personal evolution depend on our willingness to relinquish inappropriate ideas and perceptions and replace them with ones that are more correct. It is actually our strength of conviction that stunts our growth. Once again, there is weakness in strength and strength in yielding.

The task of relinquishing and revising inappropriate and erroneous views would be easy if they existed in isolation, but they do not. The psychic ecosystem is an interdependent web where the character of one image often depends on the character of another. Thus we are faced with a systemic challenge: If we are to revise or relinquish any one image, we may have to adjust an entire constellation of related images. A minor discovery might call for a complete revision of your worldview. Be prepared for this possibility.

The key to successful scientific inquiry is balance. If the imaginative voice overwhelms the critical, you become lost in a world of illusion. This is extremely dangerous; there is simply no place for untempered fantasy on the street or the battlefield. On the other hand, if the critical voice is too strong, you will generate few ideas, and those you do generate will be silenced by the internal critic. You become dull, stagnant, and vulnerable.

Create balance in this process by respecting both your critical and creative powers; allow yin and yang to alternate. When nurturing an innovative creation, withhold judgment. Move, write, speak, draw, or play with abandon. Don't be like the fledgling who defeats himself by coming up with truly novel ideas and then rejecting them instantly on "practical" grounds.

Instead, follow the path of wisdom and suspend your critical judgment. Make it a point not to reject anything, no matter how impossible it seems. Create first, then evaluate for practicality. Remember, in most situations, it only takes *one* good idea to get a resolution. Later, the voice of judgment can have its say and subject the flights of fancy to the tests of reality. That is the time for rigor, discipline, and vertical thinking.

Seek this balance continuously. Fiction, fantasy, and illusion will stimulate your creativity up to a point. Beyond that, they will distract and confuse. Temper the seduction of illusion with a quest for the truth. Fly as high as you like, but maintain contact with the ground at all times.

Be Wary of Black and White

The number two is a very dangerous number.
Attempts to divide anything in two ought to be
regarded with much suspicion.

    C. P. Snow

If you think your body and mind are two, that is
wrong; if you think that they are one, that is also
wrong. Our body and mind are both two and one.

    D. T. Suzuki

For the fledgling, most things in life are either black or white, good or evil, true or false. He puts everything in a pigeon hole: A thing either belongs to a particular class or it does not. He assumes that if something is black, it must be all black, and that nothing can be both black and white at the same time. There is no overlap between categories and there is no middle ground.

This dualistic thinking is an edged tool and, like all edged tools, it can be useful. Wielded carefully, it can help us organize our knowledge and solve practical problems. It makes perfect sense to say, "A number is *either* even *or* it is odd." But the edge of dualistic thought does not work so well in all cases; many things in this incredibly rich universe simply do not fall into neat, crisp categories.

For the owl, perfect black-and-white contrast is rare. Most relationships include degrees of harmony and conflict, health and sickness, victory and defeat, success and failure. Unfortunately, dualistic thinking gives us the illusion that a thing must be either one way or the other. By seeing things only in black and white, we miss the fantastic range of color available to us. In effect, we go blind.

The problem is not dualistic thinking itself; black-and-white distinctions do have legitimate use. If we are unwilling to wield the dualistic edge, we will procrastinate and act indecisively and eventually be defeated. The problem lies in our tendency to swing the sword of dualistic thought all around us, cutting some things well, many things poorly. We internalize the either-or orientation and use it unconsciously, thereby sabotaging our intelligence.

Dualistic thought is notorious for wreaking havoc in human relationships. Even in the best of circumstances, our relationships consist of overlapping desires, complex intentions and shifting values. But from the dualistic viewpoint, we see everything as either "for me or against me," "for us or against us." We see people either as friends or enemies, never as hybrids.

This perspective radically oversimplifies our relationships, splitting the social ecosystem into two groups, usually "us" and "them." This leads to racist, sexist, tribalistic, and nationalistic perceptions. People are either "in-group" or "out-group," "believer" or "infidel," "brother" or "other."

To make matters worse, we go on to assume that the good person or group has only "good" qualities and the "bad" person or group has only "bad" qualities. Naturally, "we" are the "good" group, the advocates of justice and truth, while "they" are the "bad" group, the evil and aggressive barbarians. From here it is just a short step to say that our behavior is "just," "reasonable," and "defensive," while theirs is "cruel," "unjustified," and "aggressive." This is the "logic" of war.

Dualistic thought distorts our worldview and cripples our conflict artistry at a fundamental level by leading us to believe that the universe is *either* friendly *or* hostile. Obviously, this does not leave us much latitude in our strategies and behaviors. We can either embrace the wonders of the universe, or we can protect ourselves from its dangers. We can either be cooperative, friendly, and trusting, or we can build a fortress of self-protection. The dualistic thinker cannot access the gray zone that is the bulk of reality; he must go forth as either a trusting, vulnerable fool with open arms, or as a grim, heavily armed warrior with a closed fist.

This approach brings nothing but trouble. Open arms and a trusting heart have their place in the owl's repertoire, but they can also lead to victimization; there are, in fact, irrational and malevolent thugs on this planet. The closed fist offers short-term security, but closes us off to the richness and benevolence of the universe.

Dualistic thinking blinds us to a whole range of tactics, including degrees of resistance, retreat, passivity, and force. It tends to obscure options such as negotiation, immobilization, nonviolent resistance, diplomacy, preemption, and education. The fledgling who limits himself exclusively to either the open embrace or the closed fist can never become an effective warrior *or* an anti-warrior.

When we think in black and white, we find it impossible to entertain opposing ideas at the same time. We come to believe that we can be either strong or sensitive, but not both. We can exercise either brains or brawn, but not both. We find it hard to imagine something that is hard-soft or strong-weak. Yet a union of complementary opposites is precisely what the aspiring owl must develop. When faced with a wide range of challenges, we need to exercise skills that are flexible-rigid, internal-external, dove-hawk, and yielding-controlled.

Since fights come in all degrees of intensity, we want our thoughts, words, and movements to be infinitely variable. Dualistic thinking makes such fine adjustments impossible. When we think in black and white, we concentrate on one extreme or another and find it impossible to make refinements that are essential to performance and artistry.

Imagine what it would be like if your face could only show two expressions, or if your body had only two postures. Imagine what it would be like if your muscles could only contract or go limp. These things strike us as absurd, unpleasant, and dangerous. So why then do we do so much of our thinking in two values? If you structure your conflict strategies as *either* fight *or* flight, you are no better off than a creature with only two expressions. If you see yourself as *either* a hawk *or* a dove, you are no better off than a body that can only contract or go slack.

Unfortunately, we are seduced into black-and-white thinking by our language. When we give something a name, we put it into a linguistic pigeonhole, believing that a thing must be in either one hole or another. This leads directly to black-and-white perceptions, judgments, and behavior. As soon as we open our mouths or put pencil to paper, we run the risk of making dualistic assumptions. In fact, conceptual pigeonholes are devices of our linguistic imagination, not actual characteristics of things or people.

Recognizing this, the owl challenges names and definitions. Be especially alert to questions and statements formed around the words "either" and "or." Be suspicious of absolutist statements that use "all," "always," "none," "never," "totally," and "completely." As author Wendell Johnson ironically put it, "Always and never are two words you should always remember never to use." Be wary of questions that demand a yes or no answer. Above all, be particularly suspicious of the word "is," a word that instantly pigeonholes a person, idea, or organization. When you hear the word "is," look for a graduated alternative.

New words are particularly helpful in transcending the limits of dualistic thinking. The Inuit people of Northern Canada have some twenty words to express relationships between the extremes of "friend" and "enemy." There is even one word that means, "I like you very much but I would not want to go seal hunting with you." Because of his superior linguistic flexibility, an Inuit is not likely to fall into a dualistic trap. Don't be a victim of a limited vocabulary. If you feel trapped by a two-valued set of words, look for new words to bridge the gap.

Transcend either-or thinking by introducing both-and phrases into your thought and speech. Integrate the spectrum. Look for sets of complementary opposites that fit together to form a single integrated whole. Acknowledge the way a person can be both friend and adversary, both smart and foolish, both compassionate and cruel, both rational and impulsive. Weapons can both start and prevent war; the universe can be both friendly and unfriendly.

Both-and reasoning stimulates creativity in all domains. Some of our most powerful ideas come to us when we struggle to hold two contrasting ideas together in a single act of perception. Both-and statements are invariably rich, challenging, and self-regulating. Thinking of things as "hard-soft," "flexible-stable," "yin-yang" is certain to rearrange static patterns and produce new leaps of insight.

If you look for dualistic qualities and characteristics, you will find them. If you look for a range of qualities and behaviors, you will find these as well. This is the difference between the fledgling and the owl. The neophyte looks at a person, process, or situation and sees only the coarsest, most obvious extremes. The owl, on the other hand, goes between the pigeonholes to find degrees of difference. Direct your attention to subtle differences and a range of qualities. Observe how the musician recognizes and appreciates a vast range of tone qualities. Observe how the photographer can see thousands of shades between light and dark. Similarly, the owl can sense and appreciate minute changes in relationship. He can tell the difference between a situation that is conflicted and another that is slightly more or less so. He is sensitive to shades of force and resistance, degrees of cooperation, and degrees of right and wrong.

There is a price to pay in this art. To transcend the dangers of dualistic thinking, you must give up a measure of apparent security, order, and certainty. A both-and world is rich and dynamic, but it can also be frightening and difficult to comprehend. To live in this multicolor zone, you must develop a high tolerance for ambiguity. Resist the temptation to revert to the simplistic, unreal world of either-or when you feel anxious or insecure. Develop a healthy relationship with the entire spectrum of your experience. Embrace a life of partial knowledge, partial control, partial friendship, partial enmity. What you give up in superficial order and security, you will more than make up for in creativity, improved performance, and rich experience.

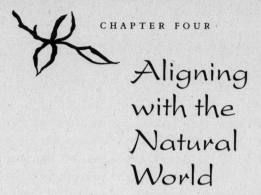

CHAPTER FOUR

Aligning with the Natural World

Think Like a Forest

Lack of systemic wisdom is always punished. If you fight the ecology of a system, you lose—especially if you "win."

Gregory Bateson

The Way of strategy is the Way of nature.

Miyamoto Musashi, *A Book of Five Rings*

The owl is an eco-warrior, intimately familiar with the characteristics of living systems and healthy organisms. He strives for an ecology of mind, body, and community. He devises conflict strategies that are appropriate to his environment. When he fights, he fights ecologically.

Rain forests, deserts, marshlands, coral reefs, and the like are not the only ecosystems. In fact, any set of relationships can be viewed in ecological terms, and common principles apply in all cases. What works in an alpine meadow also works in a marriage, a business, or a classroom.

When we take an ecological perspective, we see that all living systems are characterized by networks of interrelationships. Nothing exists in isolation; each individual is linked to all the other parts of the whole. As the first law of ecology tells us, "It's all connected."

From this perspective, the aspiring owl begins to see that all behavior reflects; attacking another person is really not much different from attacking one's self. The message comes as a variation of the golden rule. "Love thy neighbor *as* thyself" becomes "Love thy neighbor, who *is* thyself." Despite appearances to the contrary, human beings are not separate and autonomous individuals. We are connected by common physiology, experience, and a shared global predicament. Like it or not, we are one.

The first law of ecology suggests that policies of isolation and strict neutrality are fundamentally absurd. The biosphere is too interconnected for any one creature, company, or country to be an island for very long. By declaring neutrality, we give ourselves an illusion of independence and safety, but in fact we can never divorce ourselves. *Any* conflict affects us. To adopt a personal or collective policy of isolation is to say that one cell in a body can be isolated from the others and still prosper.

Everything we do has systemic consequences—all fighting behaviors have extended meaning. We cannot strike back, yield, compromise, or deceive an opponent without affecting some other part of the system. As ecologist Garrett Hardin put it, "We can never do merely one thing."

What goes around, comes around. Our conflict behaviors naturally rebound back onto us. As Lao Tzu put it, "Actions return onto one's own head." If you abuse your neighbor, or allow her to abuse you, this action reverberates throughout the social ecosystem, spreading outward through the community, and eventually returning back to you with karmic justice. As you sow the seeds of aggression and passivity, so shall you reap.

Of course, owlish behavior also has a ripple effect. Synergistic, mutually beneficial relationships echo and return as surely as any other. Thus conflict resolution is not only a good thing to do, it is also a smart thing to do. As you sow the seeds of owlish artistry, so shall you reap.

Most of us understand that our behaviors can have systemic consequences, but we often fail to appreciate just how powerful those effects can be. Complex system dynamics magnify the effects of small, apparently unimportant events. In the atmosphere, for example, small local changes in temperature or pressure can trigger massive weather systems. It is said that the flap of the butterfly's wings can set off a tornado on the other side of the planet.

Similarly, the typical human condition is highly precarious; we live our lives poised on the cusp of decision. It takes only a very small influence to motivate us in one direction or another. A wink, a nod, or a tone of voice can change the course of an entire life. Over time, small differences become big differences.

As you begin to appreciate the systemic consequences of your behavior, you will be simultaneously awed and inspired. Recognizing every behavior as potentially powerful, you will move more carefully and thoughtfully. Nothing you do is worthless, trivial, or cheap; all things, ideas, and behaviors have systemic consequence. Your power, success, and enjoyment lie in everything you touch.

Corollary: Value Diversity

As every biologist knows, one of the most important characteristics of a healthy ecosystem is diversity. A multiplicity of forms contributes to resilience and well-being in every system, whether it be a rain forest, a business, or a friendship. A family, company, or nation with diverse talents and resources is in a better position to weather the storms of an unpredictable future. The strengths of one individual are likely to compensate for weaknesses in another. There is great value in what geneticists call "hybrid vigor."

No matter what the level, the monoculture is always at risk. The monodiet leads to boredom and deficiency, the monoexercise program leads to injury, the monocurriculum leads to stagnation, narrow-mindedness, and dogma. Taken together, these add up to nutritionally deficient, injured, and closed-minded individuals, not owls.

In the ecosystem we call the human mind, diversity is equally vital. A rich variety in thoughts and images is essential to creativity, attention, and intelligence. The more diverse your mental environment, the more alternatives you can wield. Options allow freedom, empowerment, relaxation, and higher overall performance. Thus diversity equals power.

Naturally, the owl values diversity in his martial philosophy. He would never wish for a monoculture of hawks or doves—a changing environment could wipe out the entire system. The fledgling bashes the aggressiveness of hawks or ridicules the naiveté of doves, failing to realize that *both* perspectives are essential and that a diversity of thought will actually strengthen our practice of personal, organizational, and international conflict artistry. We need both hawks and doves in our personalities.

Eschew the monoculture. Cross-train in all dimensions of your experience. Diversify your knowledge, skills, and relationships. Make your study multidisciplinary as you develop a repertoire of images, ideas, and concepts. The day may come when the offbeat, unusual, or conflicting idea may prove to be indispensable.

Corollary: Self-Regulate

Another essential characteristic of living systems is the ability to self-regulate. The healthy organism knows how to maintain a stable internal equilibrium in the face of constant external change. The good animal regulates blood temperature, pressure, and chemical concentrations at nearly constant levels despite large fluctuations in environmental conditions.

Self-regulation is the product of opposing forces. In the animal body, for example, two sets of muscles lie across every joint, one a prime mover and the other antagonistic to it. When one muscle contracts, the limb will move in that direction unless it is opposed by a contraction on the opposite side. Contraction of the antagonistic muscle limits and regulates. This makes for smooth and graceful movement.

Without opposition, even the simplest movement would require extraordinary levels of concentration. We would find it nearly impossible to pick up a pencil, turn the pages in a book, or draw a picture. If we attempted any vigorous movement, our limbs would destroy themselves with radically unstable spasm and oscillation.

A system without an antagonist is impossible to regulate and will inevitably go to self-destructive extremes. Thus every idea needs a negative, every culture a counterculture, every government a loyal opposition. The sound of one wing flapping is the sound of a system in imminent danger.

Up to a point, opposition is perfectly ecological. It regulates motion, stimulates growth, and maintains equilibrium. That which opposes us also nourishes us. For the aspiring owl, this knowledge is liberating. As soon as you recognize the value in opposition, you are less likely to resist it and more likely to make creative use of it. You may even come to relish it. Your opponent may actually be an ally in your quest to survive and prosper.

Since both sides in a conflicted relationship regulate one another, destruction of either one will adversely affect the entire system. Extremely hawkish strategies aimed at annihilation of an opponent are usually nonecological and may contribute to the early death of both parties. At the same time, extremely dovish strategies of passivity are also nonecological. Thus the owl does not attempt to destroy his opponent, nor does he allow his opponent to destroy him. From the ecological perspective, conflict art succeeds by "not winning, not losing."

The owl's objective is not to eliminate conflict or achieve a perfect peace, but to fine-tune his resistance to support the health of both his own interests and the ecosystem as a whole. He wants to engage in a mutually beneficial struggle, not senseless confrontation.

In opposing the excesses of others, we provide an essential ecological service. In fact, it is our ecological responsibility to oppose and regulate the behavioral extremes around us. The trick, of course, is to oppose the right things with the optimal degree of resistance. Not all actions of other people or groups require opposition; the owl does not oppose others indiscriminately. Rather, he acts with systemic awareness and intelligence.

Be selective. Limit your opponent's tendency to go to extremes. Temper her inclination to put the entire system at risk. Observe the health of the system and its tendency to move toward excess. Look for positive feedback spirals, processes that tend to escalate or feed off themselves. If you see something becoming unstable or growing out of control, move to oppose it. Look for trends; anything that is on an exponential curve is immediately suspect!

Corollary: Play the Rhythms

As a conflict ecologist, the owl is keenly aware of the periodic oscillation that defines every healthy ecosystem. From the cyclical movement of subatomic particles to the breathing of animals to the tides and seasons, cycles and rhythm pervade every aspect of life. We eat and sleep, work and play, talk and listen, train and rest. These things are like our breath, the primordial rhythm: They rise, climax, fall away, and return again.

Integrate your behavior with these rhythms; breathe these patterns as you would your own inhalations and exhalations. If you are learning a new discipline, alternate periods of intense concentration with periods of relaxation and play. Alternate periods of intimacy with periods of independence. Alternate times of action with times of contemplation.

Breathe your behavior. Make smooth transitions from one phase to another and strive for full expression of each phase. If you are breathing a work-play cycle or a rational-intuitive cycle, ease gently from one phase to the other, while doing each as vigorously as possible. Holding on to one phase for too long is the equivalent of holding your breath: possible, but something that must ultimately give way.

Human relationship also shows periodic, oscillating behavior. The fledgling assumes that his conflicted relationships follow a strict pattern of cause and effect, but this may not be the case at all.

Human conflict and resolution may actually come and go ecologically, like the phases of the moon or the changes in the weather, with or without our conscious interference. Fights and arguments arise periodically and without provocation, sparked by trivial causes. The storm rages, and then suddenly the wind dies down and calm returns. All of this seems to transpire in spite of our efforts to the contrary. We think we are in control of the process, but perhaps we are just living out a natural cycle.

Look for cyclic oscillation in the resistance that you face. Perhaps your conflict is simply part of a systemic rhythm that will resolve itself naturally. Perhaps interference will only upset the natural process that is already underway beneath the surface. Open yourself to the rhythmic functioning of the system as a whole; play the yin with patience and reserve. By simply waiting, a conflict may run its course naturally.

Corollary: Conserve

As that great owl Heraclitus might have told us, "You can't step into the same ecosystem twice." Things change; an enemy today may be an ally tomorrow. What angers us today may enlighten us tomorrow. Acknowledge this dynamic quality by never doing more damage in a conflict than necessary. Total annihilation of an opponent may satisfy your primal urges for revenge, but this is foolishness, not artistry. Sun Tzu emphasized this course:

> To capture the enemy's army is better than to destroy it; to take intact a battalion, a company, or a five-man squad is better than to destroy them.

The owl appreciates change. He sees alliances and conditions in flux all around him and has no desire to close off options or commit to an irrevocable course of action. He lives on options and alternatives and so keeps them open as long as possible. Since he doesn't know what may be useful in the future, he conserves—not just human life, but property, ideas, philosophies, cultures, relationships, species, and ecosystems as well. As conservationist Aldo Leopold put it, "The first rule of intelligent tinkering is to save all the cogs and wheels." Don't burn bridges unless you have no other choice.

Corollary: Participate

The best way to learn the lessons of the natural world is through direct experience and participation. Unfortunately, we often neglect this path. Our culture seeks separation from the natural world, and much of our knowledge comes about, not by way of experience and contact, but by distance and separation. This gives us power and control, but at an enormous cost of isolation and alienation. This strategy is the polar opposite of animal epistemology, in which creatures know the world precisely by putting themselves in direct sensory contact with it.

We cannot learn the lessons of nature when we stand apart. We must immerse ourselves in the living world. As the Zen poet Basho put it, "To learn about the pine, go to the pine. To learn about the bamboo, go to the bamboo." Participation means touching and smelling and hearing the living earth. It means getting intimate with the forest and the desert and the ocean. It means rubbing your nose in the wild. It means getting wet, dirty, cold, hungry, lost, and completely exhausted.

Economic culture teaches us that "escape" to the wild is selfish, but nothing could be further from the truth. In fact, going to the wild is a socially responsible, therapeutic act of high order. Participation dissolves the human-nature duality and teaches us in ways that can never be approached in the civilized world.

Do not neglect this practice. Immerse yourself in the wild; engage the living world in a dialogue. Get as far from the road as you possibly can. Experience the wonders of diversity, regulation, and adaptation in your own body. Listen to the language of evolution. This is important work.

Honor the Game

We should fight to check the enemy, not eliminate him. We
must learn to include ourselves in the round of cooperations
and conflicts, of symbiosis and preying, which constitutes
the balance of nature, for a permanently victorious species
destroys, not only itself, but all other life in its environment.

Alan Watts, *The Book*

All healthy ecophysiologies obey the laws of rock–scissors–paper. This
is a game of circular influence in which each player wields partial
power and control. Rock smashes scissors, but can be covered by paper. Paper covers rock, but can be cut by scissors. Scissors cuts paper,
but can be smashed by rock. Any species can be overcome by any
other. There is no ultimate dominant, no perfect alpha. Even the top
predators may be overcome by microorganisms, asteroids, climatic
changes, or scarcity of food. In this sense, all species are equal.

The problem comes when we resist the nature of the game. Not
content with an occasional victory, the fledgling tries to rig the game
so that he is always alpha. In search of perfect security, he looks for
strategies and technologies that will guarantee a consistently positive
outcome. He builds new weapons, sends out agents, launches satellites,
and squeezes his domestic life for every possible defensive resource. He
aspires to be the rock that can beat both paper and scissors.

The consequence of this effort is not difficult to imagine—short-
term success that leads to ultimate defeat. If rock does manage to beat
paper, the game is over; the balance that made the game so wonderful
is now destroyed and there is no longer any game to play.

Obviously, every species and individual must strive for some level
of influence and control in its environment. The owl must protect his

legitimate niche; rock should beat scissors, scissors should beat paper. But if our influence grows too great, the entire structure of the game breaks down and we go with it. If paper managed to beat scissors as well as rock, the game would be worthless as a self-regulating organism. If we win a little, we win. But if we win big, we lose everything.

Respect the rock-scissors-paper nature of healthy ecosystems by practicing restraint, moderation, humility, and a low profile. Take your victories where you can, but stay within your niche. Do not aspire to do more than what you do well. Do not aspire to domination or total security. Be content with partial power and partial influence, just as any good animal would be. By participating in the play but not dominating it, you can enjoy the whole game. The owl doesn't need to rule the forest to thrive in it.

Walk Softly

When faced with hostile threats, many of us wish that we could become invisible. We think, "If my adversary can't see me, he can't attack me. If he can't attack me, he can't hurt me. If I am invisible, I am safe."

In some ways, this stealth strategy is a good one. Stealth is common in the animal world, and many creatures survive by keeping a low profile. Anonymity is economical: It is far less expensive to avoid a fight through stealth than it is to risk injury or death in an unpredictable battle.

In general, there is little to be gained by drawing unnecessary attention to yourself. Therefore, the owl maintains a low profile by blending body and behavior into his surroundings. He touches the world gently and leaves little trace of his passage. He moves as gently as Sun Tzu's "ghost in the starlight."

Fundamental as it is, stealth is not infallible, nor is it appropriate for all situations. Excess blending leads us into a new context. We begin by changing our speech, our clothing, and our views. We keep a low profile by being obedient to authority and complying with the dominant ideological paradigm; we seek safety in anonymity. Eventually, our stealth strategy becomes unconscious and we live a lifestyle devoted not only to physical invisibility, but to social and political invisibility as well.

This compulsive blending exacts a heavy cost, however. When we commit to stealth, we sacrifice personal expression and creativity; we give up options and power. Moreover, a state of apparent safety may be an illusion; constantly going with the flow can make you safe from immediate attack, but this advantage disappears if the flow itself is moving toward danger or chaos.

Stealth and conformity also transform our sense of responsibility. When in the presence of authority, disobedience makes us visible and vulnerable, so we do what we are told and don't ask questions. This pleases the bosses, but opens the door to the dangers of groupthink. If people are compulsively hiding, those in power can direct them in any direction they wish, however ill-conceived or barbaric. Ultimately, compulsive invisibility leads to social decay and atrocity. If everyone in a group is practicing stealth, no one will be taking risks, venturing opinions or taking on challenges. If everyone is practicing invisibility, no one is safe.

In spite of these dangers, treading gently remains a sound strategy and an essential part of an owlish repertoire. The objective is consciousness. If you choose to glide quietly, do it with awareness. If you choose stealth, do it intentionally and sparingly, not out of compulsion. Be versatile. Learn how to become invisible and how to stand out.

Travel Light

> To live within limits, to want one thing, or a very few
> things, very much and love them dearly, cling to them,
> survey them from every angle, become one with them—
> that is what makes the poet, the artist, the human being.
>
> Johann Wolfgang von Goethe

> Lives based on having are less free than lives based on
> either doing or being.
>
> William James

Life and battle conditions change constantly. The owl must be highly mobile; she may have to adapt or change position on a moment's notice. If she is pinned down by a heavy load of physical or psychological possessions, however, she will be stuck. Dead weight will make her vulnerable and ineffective.

The fledgling believes that by accumulating possessions, she is accumulating power. She spends enormous effort gathering material goods in the belief that they will give her more control and security. Up to a point, this approach succeeds, but as usual, the extreme reverses itself. Too many attachments—to things, ideas, or behaviors—will eventually destroy her mobility. The materialistic warrior is ultimately more vulnerable, not less.

In contrast, the owl is skeptical of her possessions. She understands that, in many circumstances, power can be measured not by what she has, but by what she is able to do without. Follow this path. Limit your quest for acquisition. Question your possessions and practice going light. If you can gain power by acquiring tools and materials, do it, but do not allow them to become your masters. Be prepared to abandon them as soon as they outlive their usefulness or interfere with your movement. In the end, your owlhood will be measured by the quality of your action, not by the magnitude of your fortune. The more you give up, the less you have to lose and the more powerful you can be.

Carry a Small Stick

Let your own discretion be your tutor; suit the action to the word, the word to the action; with this special observance, that you o'erstep not the modesty of nature.

Shakespeare

Art is about quality, but it is also about quantity, scale, and proportion; it is a search for the right amount. Whether it be the right amount of paint or light or sound, art consistently asks the question, "How much?"

This search for the perfect quantity reflects the ways of nature. In any ecosystem, there is an ideal level for every substance. Too little oxygen in the earth's atmosphere and life would perish; too much and fires would break out everywhere. Minerals are essential in the animal diet, but in high concentrations they become poisonous.

The study of optimal levels is central in the science of toxicology. For the toxicologist, no substance is inherently toxic or polluting; what matters is the amount. A glass of wine with dinner may be therapeutic, but beyond that you take your chances. As the saying goes, "The dose makes the poison."

When the level of a substance increases beyond the optimal level, there is often a dramatic reversal of function. A small amount of food gives us energy, a large amount makes us lazy and tired. A small amount of stress focuses our attention and improves our performance, but a large amount distracts us and weakens our powers. A mild sedative may become a stimulant if given in a large dose, and vice versa. The extreme leads to its opposite.

The same holds true in the realm of defense. As more weapons are added to a system and more attention is paid to defense, the payoff begins to reverse itself. Beyond a certain point, more defense results in less security. If the process continues, large amounts of defense will actually make a person or an organization more vulnerable than if they had not defended themselves in the first place.

This principle operates in all social ecosystems from the micro to the macro. The man who simply locks his doors and keeps an eye out for trouble will realize a significant increase in security. If he owns a dog, even more so. If he owns a weapon, perhaps an even greater increase. But beyond this, he begins to experience diminishing returns; two weapons will not make him twice as secure, three weapons will not make him three times as secure.

When the fledgling sets out to defend himself, he finds that his first efforts give him an increased sense of security. Since he is initially successful in his effort, he comes to the conclusion that security and defense share a direct relationship. He thinks, "If some defense is good, more must be better."

In fact, defense and security do not share a direct and linear relationship. Low levels of defense initially bring large gains in security, but this advantage eventually falls off. At some point, the fledgling's increase in security will reverse itself and his defense will become self-defeating.

Excess defense defeats its purpose in three ways. In the first place, it pollutes human ecosystems with fear and anxiety, which generates reactive defense, which causes more fear and reactivity. Paradoxically, defenses tend to create what they were designed to defend against—we find that we need more defense to defend against the results of our defense.

A high level of defense also defeats its purpose when it deprives us of resources that might otherwise be used for health, education, or self-care. Beyond the optimal, defense becomes parasitic, feeding on the vitality of the organism it was designed to protect. The fledgling who spends all his time looking over his shoulder and honing his sword won't have time to read books, play music, make friends, or nurture his personal health. He may be safe from external threats, but his internal environment will be so shallow and undernourished that it will scarcely be worth defending anyway.

The practice of defense can stimulate attention and intelligence, but only up to a point. Beyond that, it obscures the path to enlightenment and becomes a form of anti-education. A strong defense offers short-term protection but long-term stagnation, maladjustment, and paradoxically, increased vulnerability. In the extreme, defense can make us stupid.

Thus the owl seeks an optimal level of defense continuously. Study the extremes and narrow your focus. If you find yourself victimized by hostile forces, increase the yang. If you find that your defensive efforts are poisoning the local ecosystem or drawing off resources from domestic or personal needs, increase the yin. Of course, optimal defense is not a static quantity; since your environment is always changing, you will have to make constant adjustments.

It is relatively easy to increase defensive efforts and build more weapons. The more difficult challenge is to reduce our defenses. We believe that if we soften our position, our opponents will rush in to destroy us (our opponents, of course, think the same thing). Thus we buttress our defenses further, ignoring the fact that less defense might actually make us safer and more secure. Of course the prospect is risky. But which risk is greater? The possibility that an opponent will attack, or the certainty that continued high levels of defense will pollute the entire system and bankrupt us domestically? Taking the risk is often the safest course.

Seek Balance

An elevated spirit is weak and a low spirit is weak.

Miyamoto Musashi, *A Book of Five Rings*

Thus a master of any art avoids excess and deficit,
but seeks the intermediate and chooses this.

Aristotle

Gliding silently through the night air, the owl listens closely to the subtle messages from his inner ear, wings, and torso, making constant adjustments. The wind may be turbulent but his concentration remains focused. He makes tiny corrections with tail and wing tips, sculpting the air in every moment. His flight is a balancing act.

Balance is essential for defense, ecological relationship, and intelligent creation. Without a sense of proportion, you cannot hope to harness your power. Moreover, you become vulnerable. Your opponents will take advantage of your instability and throw you to the ground.

In the balanced animal, yin and yang complete each other to form a dynamic unity. The yang is active and direct, powerful and controlling. With this influence, we take charge of our lives and overcome our doubts and insecurities. We move and instigate. We define boundaries and make decisions; we just do it.

On the other side is the yin, the yielding and receptive. Here we make internal adjustments and adapt to conditions that we don't like or cannot change. We become like water, adapting our shape and attitude without resistance; we let it be.

Yang without yin is dangerous, as is yin without yang. Too much yin and you will fail to accomplish your goals; people and organizations will walk all over you. Too much yang and you will become aggressive, pushy, and domineering. You will develop an alpha male, alpha female, top-of-the-food-chain personality. You will alienate and abuse your fellows.

Thus the owl trains for both yin and yang behaviors. An ambidextrous artist, he uses one wing for self-protection and the other for embrace. He is neither the abuser nor the abused, neither the destroyer nor the destroyed. He takes care of his own interests and territory without victimizing others. He is neither passive nor aggressive, but assertive.

Honor both sides of the challenges that you face and seek equitable proportion at every possible level. Look for the golden mean between order and chaos, freedom and discipline, the practical and the ideal, conservation and innovation, purposeful activity and contemplation, the spiritual and the secular, planning and improvisation, obedience and independence, strength and flexibility, the classical and the romantic.

The curious thing about balance is that while it must be sought, it can never be achieved. If everything stayed still, achieving balance would be relatively easy. We could simply measure the excesses and deficiencies and even them out. But since the world is always in motion, balance can never be complete or final. Like birds in flight, we always have to adjust for new conditions. Every state of equilibrium is provisional. No structure, process, or relationship is completely stable. Thus the owl is vigilant in adjusting the need for force and for restraint.

This art is subtle. Caught in the midst of myriad forces, most of our action is based on partial knowledge and understanding. We don't always know where the center lies or even whether we are headed in the right direction. When we are off balance, an impulsive correction might just make things worse.

Under these conditions, the owlish strategy is to make small corrections in course and intensity. This approach has several advantages. If you make a large correction, even in the right direction, you may radically overshoot the mark and wind up even further off balance than when you began. Observe how the fledgling nervously oscillates from one overcorrection to another, always hunting for the big fix that will provide security. First he chooses a path of strength and inflexible power. When that fails he switches to being accommodating and passive. When that fails, he returns to his original style with renewed intensity. In the end, he is neither an effective hawk nor a successful dove. Small corrections, on the other hand, are easy to control, easy to monitor, and do not carry nearly as much risk.

In all cases, balance is best achieved without leaning. The creature that is consistently leaning on things around him will never develop a honed sense of equilibrium. In leaning, he commits his motion to a single direction and loses versatility and dexterity. His support may give way unexpectedly or be knocked down by a clever opponent. If he is suddenly attacked, he may find it difficult to adjust.

Leaning is a poor tactic because it deprives us of valuable feedback and experience. When we rely on external support, there is no longer any challenge to our normal balancing skills. By borrowing strength from an external source, the fledgling builds weakness and trains for dependence. The more he leans on substances, processes, or people, the weaker he becomes.

The challenge is to stand erect. Resist the temptation to lean, particularly when you are under stress or heavily challenged. Eliminate every possible crutch. Seek self-sufficiency and upright integration at all times. Of course, there is a point of optima here. Don't deprive yourself of rest when you are tired or injured. Use props as necessary, but return to your balanced stance at the earliest opportunity.

Balance would seem to be a skill beyond question, but even this quest can be carried to extremes. In ignorance and confusion, the fledgling compulsively splits the difference on every issue and ends up living on the fence, secure but without passion, balanced but without motivation. Coming down in the middle becomes a reactive habit, a stealth defense. Here the fledgling becomes a passive neutralist, trying to hide in the middle by declaring moderation on every issue. At the very least, this compulsive balancing act eventually makes life bland, static, and boring. In contrast, a system that is slightly off balance has the potential for high energy and rapid, adaptive movement. Balancing is a high virtue, but it is not the only virtue. Sometimes the owl must go to the extremes. Be balanced about balance.

CHAPTER FIVE

Training the Mind's Eye

*The mind of the general ought
to resemble and be as clear as the
field glass of a telescope.*

NAPOLEON BONAPARTE

*"Are you a god?" they asked
the Buddha.
  "No."
"An angel?"
  "No."
"A saint?"
  "No."
"Then what are you?"
  "I am awake."*

Refine Your Sensitivity

To distinguish between the sun and the moon
is no test of vision; to hear the thunderclap is
no indication of acute hearing.

Sun Tzu

When engaging the opposition, it is a matter of supreme importance to see things as they really are. Superior technique means nothing if you don't see an attack coming. Awareness is the crucial element.

The owl, of course, is a bird of extreme sensitivity. Because she sees and hears the subtle changes in her environment, she can act early, before her options begin to narrow. Since she can feel the true character of a situation, she can devise a response that fits.

In contrast, the fledgling's primary strategy is to insulate himself from the dangerous and threatening aspects of his environment. When something hurts, he desensitizes himself with layers of psychophysical insulation and buffers. This protects him from unpleasant sensation, but it also makes it difficult for him to feel, see, and hear the subtle qualities of his experience. What he gains in protection is offset by huge losses in somatic intelligence.

Beyond the optimal, defense and sensitivity share an inverse relationship. The more we defend ourselves with blocking, fortification, or armoring, the less we will know about our environment and the resistance that we face. The extreme leads to its opposite. Desensitized by compulsive defensiveness, we lose the very information and knowledge we need to effectively defend ourselves.

The owl counters this tendency by stripping away her insulation and armor to the lowest possible level. By opening herself up to her environment and experience, she gains sensitivity and essential knowledge. She makes herself vulnerable to make herself safe.

Owlish sensitivity is best developed in an atmosphere of simplicity and scarcity. Quiet, in all its forms, is essential. Just as soft sounds become audible as background noise begins to fade, so too do other senses become sharper in relative quiet. Thus the owl seeks visual-quiet, touch-quiet, smell-quiet, taste-quiet, and emotional-quiet. Position yourself in silent regions of experience where you will hear more, see more, feel more, smell more, and taste more. Listen for whispers, feel the microscopic, and look for the imperceptible.

Play with the limits. Just how sensitive can a nerve cell be? Can you see a single photon or smell a single molecule of your favorite food? Strive for a breadth and depth of sensitivity; specialize in one discipline and feel for the finest possible variation, then generalize for a variety of sensation.

The vital ingredient for developing sensitivity is time. Extended sensory contact is essential for seeing, feeling, and hearing the finer shades of experience. Speed blinds us, deafens us, and numbs us. In fact, the fledgling often hurries for precisely this reason. He discovers that he can protect himself from uncomfortable sensations by moving fast. In contrast, the owl lingers, keeping his senses in contact with his environment, even when it is unpleasant. He speeds up if the situation demands it, but then slows again to reestablish sensory connection. Be your own ally in this process; practice your art at a leisurely pace.

Acute sensitivity springs from a healthy animal body. Work with raw physical reality as often as possible. Nothing will sharpen your senses like a genuine threat to survival. Comfort dulls our sight, our hearing, our sense of taste and smell. Risk, on the other hand, sensitizes us. If you want to hear more, feel more, and see more, expose yourself.

Naturally, your sensitivity will wax and wane like the tides and the seasons. On some days you will be able to see and feel the most delicate qualities; on others, even the coarsest contrasts will seem inaccessible. Accept this dynamic. Be sensitive to your own sensitivity. When you are one with the task, press on to greater challenges; when you are dull to your art, move with caution and reserve.

Lead with imagination. Can you hear the sound of distant footsteps? Can you see the glow of a human heart? The narrowing of your partner's eyes? Can you feel the sap running in the trees? The growing power of a storm? The movements of the earth? The spark of a single nerve cell? At first you sense nothing, but eventually the faint will soon become obvious, the fine coarse, and the whisper a roar. By attending to the subtle, you will make yourself safe and effective.

See What You Look At

When facing a single tree, if you look at a single one of its leaves, you will not see all the others. If a single leaf holds the eye, it will be as if the remaining leaves were not there.

Takuan Soho, *The Unfettered Mind*

In spite of his extraordinary sensitivity, even the most experienced owl does not perceive reality directly. He selects and filters experience through his nervous system, language, and unconscious assumptions. His mind attends to certain things while disregarding others. Even under the best of conditions, all he sees is a glimpse of the totality. No single creature can absorb all there is to see, hear, or feel.

The human mind protects itself from anxiety by contracting awareness. When we feel threatened or insecure, we narrow our attention to reduce our awareness of the threat. This process operates unconsciously, just as the iris of the eye contracts when the light gets brighter. Unfortunately, the fledgling is ignorant of this process. He assumes that he has direct access to reality, and so is completely unaware of his limited awareness. He is blind to his own blindness.

To a certain extent, this filtering process is necessary. If our attention were open to everything that is potentially threatening, we would be overwhelmed by a flood of sensation. By limiting what we attend to, we feel more secure and therefore more functional. But this process of restricting awareness involves a trade-off, and it is only adaptive up to a point. If we contract our awareness too drastically or too frequently, we lose touch with our environment and become blind to genuine dangers.

The first rule of attention is this: We don't see what we look *at*, we see what we look *for*. Expectation directs attention. We see what we expect to see. If you expect to see a friendly universe around you, you will probably see compassion, altruism, and good humor. If you expect a hostile universe, you will probably see violence, selfishness, and treachery. Anticipation distorts perception. Previewing distorts viewing.

The owlish solution to selective attention is disinterest. If we are not interested in a particular thing, we will not be looking for it, and thus our minds will be open to anything that might happen. Here there is no inclination, no tendency, and no bias, not even toward beauty, goodness, or excellence. Disinterest is the attitude of no-attitude. As Confucius would have put it, "The owl does not set his mind either for anything or against anything." He watches and observes openly; he does not look for any particular quality or any particular event. He has no preference and no agenda. The owl is just plain interested.

This disinterested state of mind is unfamiliar to many of us. We are, after all, educated. Our teachers spend years directing our attention to particular qualities, events, and places. This guidance is useful in developing specialized skills, but this is different from the disinterested mental state of the owl, scientist, detective, or Zen master.

Paradoxically, education can skew our attention just as effectively as ignorance. Knowledge is not always an ally. Training and discipline channel attention and build expectation; this becomes a source of both power and limitation. To see with clarity, you must be willing to abandon not only your ignorance, bias, and prejudice, but your most precious insights and hard-won realizations as well. To see clearly, you must suspend it all. Assume no knowledge. The mature owl must have the openness of a fledgling.

To see with disinterest, you must be able to separate yourself, at least temporarily, from the passions, fears, and emotions that drive and color your attention. Obviously, this can become excessive; there is a need for eco-logic. The owl does not divorce himself completely from his emotional life, but he can hold it in reserve to achieve a dispassionate view.

View with intense and passionate disinterest. Look at familiar things as if you had never seen them before. In all moments, stay mindful of your limited awareness! Never assume that you have the complete story. Never assume that you see the whole picture. There is always more. Keep looking.

Keep the Scan Going

When the mind stops, it will be grasped by the opponent.

Takuan Soho, *The Unfettered Mind*

In her powers of dynamic awareness, the owl is a master of the scan. By moving her attention smoothly and continuously, she builds up a comprehensive image of her situation. She gathers information broadly, deeply, and without prejudice and assembles it into a coherent whole.

There are two errors we can make in the scanning process: fixation and omission. When we fixate, our attention congeals on a single aspect of our environment, relationship, or predicament. When we omit, we avoid looking at things we need to see.

Fixation and omission are universal errors in human attention, closely related to the twin behaviors of addiction and aversion. Addiction is fixation, an error of attention. The fledgling who fixates is suffering from a form of micro-addiction. Aversion is the complementary error. It is the blind spot in attention, the place we are afraid to look. It is our denial, our refusal to face a particular aspect of our predicament.

Ideally, our scans ought to be smooth, methodical, and comprehensive. What actually happens, of course, is that we become distracted by anxiety and desire. Instead of absorbing without prejudice, our scans become rough, jerky, and fitful. As we fixate and avoid, the scan becomes sticky and fragmented. At this point, our composite pictures of reality begin to lose their accuracy and we become vulnerable.

Fixation is especially deadly when we are under attack. In combat and in life, it is essential that the mind be present in the moment, not detained elsewhere. When someone lashes out in our direction, our first inclination is to focus on the threat, a thoroughly adaptive response. But when focus becomes fixation, we begin to obsess on the attack and pay less mind to other aspects of our environment. Ironically, excess attention to the attack can actually prevent us from exercising a creative defense.

Omission is equally dangerous. If you deny the existence of a threat, you may miss the attack and get blindsided. The fledgling believes that "what you can't see won't hurt you," but it is precisely the thing that he won't look at that will strike him down.

A quality scan is a fragile creature. Stress, fear, and anger narrow the breadth of the scan and we see less. This, of course, makes error and frustration more likely, which reduces the breadth of the scan still further. Since our vision is restricted, we are more vulnerable than before and it is likely that we will encounter even more trouble, which reduces our awareness even further.

Recognizing this, the owl's primary goal is to keep the scan going. Keep your awareness extended, even in the midst of chaos. Look around corners and into the shadows. Even as problems or distractions develop, keep your attention moving. If you find your mind lingering in one place, move on. If you begin to feel the stickiness and fixation of an addiction, however small, return to the broader scan. If you notice that you are failing to notice something, slow down and give it the attention it deserves.

If your scan does begin to break down in the face of stress or confusion, simplify your task and slow down. Ignore all nonessentials, trivial amusements, and distractions. As the situation becomes more challenging, intensify your discipline. Limit your scan strictly to fundamentals. Once you have gained control over the process, you may broaden the scope of your attention, but continue to monitor. As soon as you begin to fixate or omit, drop back to simplicity. With practice, you will learn to recognize fixation and omission at earlier stages and overcome them more easily.

No matter what the situation, monitor your scan continuously. Watch your watching, mind your minding. What catches your eye? How long does it linger? Is it difficult to drag yourself away? What won't you look at? How far out of your way will you go to avoid looking at those things that make you fearful, uncomfortable, or anxious? Pay attention to what you pay attention to.

Of course, excessive attention to the errors in your scan is itself a fixation. If you do get stuck, don't get stuck on that fact. Fixating on the fact that you are fixated is the beginning of a particularly vicious spiral. Let it go.

Focus

One has to learn to regulate one's attention.... An overall view of the board is built up gradually by switching one's concentration from one section of the battle to another.

Nikolai Krogius, *Psychology in Chess*

Highly focused concentration is essential to success in all aspects of life, art, and combat. Only by bringing our powers of attention into harmonious union can we hope to perform at a high level. Unfortunately, the fledgling finds this state elusive; he falls in and out of focused concentration at random and has little control over the process. The owl, on the other hand, follows a deliberate and intentional method to cultivate this state.

Begin with your environment. If possible, your place of practice should be clean, simple, and easily manageable; an island of order in the midst of an otherwise chaotic world. Simple surroundings will encourage the extension and refinement of your senses. Be your own ally in this process; set up your environment so that there will be as few distractions as possible; details are crucial.

When beginning your practice, do not attempt to jump directly into a state of focused concentration. Gather your intensity gradually. Observe a ritual or routine to bring your attention into focus. Bow to the mat, sharpen your tools, tune your instrument, or don the appropriate clothing. These preparations speak to the unconscious and set the transformation in motion. Whatever your chosen discipline, establish a focusing sequence and honor it.

Once you have made a transition into the zone of focused concentration, maintain it with as much purity as possible. If you find your concentration wavering, gently coax it back onto target. If you are unsuccessful, intensify your effort, but only to the point of optima. If this fails, consider stopping the activity altogether. Do not train yourself in error. It is better to exercise short periods of high-quality concentration than long periods of fragmented and frustrated effort. Monitor your focus and honor the point when it starts to fade.

If possible, penetrate directly to the very center of your task. If this proves impossible, enter obliquely. Sneak into it laterally. Spiral your attention into focus, cutting down the distractions a little at a time. Force is rarely effective in establishing or maintaining concentration. Far better to fall into it as if by accident. Power your effort, not with an aggressive will, but with fascination and involvement; seduce yourself into focus. As your curiosity becomes engaged, you will become one with the task.

Since the objective is pure concentration, some might assume that there is no room for distraction in this art. This is not exactly the case. When focused, the owl is not locked onto his target objective; his concentration is strong, but remains flexible. After all, a distraction might signal a more compelling challenge that must take priority; focus must be adaptive. Since we live in a dynamic environment, some level of distraction is inevitable and healthy. Select as you must, but don't worry a great deal about distraction. The enemies of concentration are persistent, cunning, and thrive on resistance. Do not encourage them with opposition—they will only increase in strength. Let them come and let them go. Don't give them more power than they already have.

Cycle

The natural remedy is to be found in the proportion
which the night bears to the day, the winter to summer,
thought to experience.

Henry David Thoreau

Some people imagine the owl as a neo-samurai warrior-athlete who is always on full alert, a creature with perfect posture, fluid breathing, and continually extended awareness. They imagine someone who lives in a state of perfect combat readiness, always in the here and now.

In theory, this moment-to-moment mobilization is sound practice. After all, there is no way to predict when an attack might come; if we could be fully alert at all times, we would be safe. Nevertheless, the idea of continuous mobilization violates ecological principles of rhythm and cyclic movement. Striving to be constantly "on" is like trying to hold your breath all day or wishing that the earth would hold a fixed position in its orbit around the sun. In practice, the extreme of constant mobilization ultimately gives way to its opposite: distraction and disintegration.

As always, there is an optimal point of function that we must observe. Clearly, most of us could benefit from better moment-to-moment attention to breathing, posture, and environment. Most of us ought to spend more time in the here and now. But at the same time, every creature needs time to regenerate and play with distraction. Anything static makes us vulnerable. To strive for higher levels of attention and psychophysical mobilization is a worthy goal, but to strive for constantly focused attention may be an error. Just as the body needs periods of rest, so too does the power of attention.

Build some cyclic rhythm into your awareness and lifestyle. Focus and release your mind. Move back and forth between freedom and discipline, romance and rigor, easy wandering and intentional action. Intensify and relinquish your awareness as conditions change. Create a state of consciousness that is mobilized, dynamic, and sustainable.

Be simultaneously cautious and curious, wary and relaxed. Sustain those qualities that are useful in combat and in daily life: alertness, sensitivity, balance, intensity, and integration. Find the proportion of martial awareness and intention that is appropriate for your environment.

Live a yin-yang cycle of attention, but keep your martial skills and capabilities readily accessible. Don't get too far from the here and now. Even when you are in the midst of full yin rejuvenation, be prepared to make a smooth and instantaneous transition to "full alert" status if the situation demands it. Be a good animal in this regard; keep your skills and intensity close to the surface so that you can access them on a moment's notice. There is no way of telling when a challenge or attack might materialize.

CHAPTER SIX

The Way That Can Be Spoken Of

Travel the Territory

> I can't remember not being suspicious of words. I treat them as I do any approaching shadows on a half-lit street in a city.
>
> T. E. Tucker

The fledgling is apathetic about language. He treats symbols carelessly, spewing them out as if they were cheap and harmless. In fact, they are neither. Words that distort, mislead, or dehumanize are extremely dangerous.

The owl is a semantic artist, a linguistic warrior. She appreciates the power of language and uses it in the same way that she would use a sword or any other sharp instrument: with profound respect.

As the prime mover of human intelligence, language shapes nearly every dimension of our experience. As semanticist Wendell Johnson put it, "We see with our categories." Words direct our attention, our perceptions, and consequently our behavior. Because it shapes the way we think, language also contributes to our psychic ecology. Language can be a great ally or a subversive enemy.

The owl views language as if it were a map, a symbolic guide to the territory that she would like to travel. The purpose of this linguistic map is to show the prominent features of the terrain so that we may navigate effectively from place to place. Maps are interesting in and of themselves, but the owl's primary interest lies in the territory that the map is supposed to represent.

The master principle of cartography and navigation is that the map is not the territory—that is, the word is not the thing. If you draw a map of a mountain range, you might use a triangle to represent a mountain, but that triangle is not the mountain. You might use a line to represent a river, but that line is not the river.

Human beings choose symbols to represent objects, processes, and ideas, but our choice of symbols is arbitrary. There is no necessary connection between a symbol and the thing it is intended to represent. The meaning is not in the symbol, it is in the person, the user of the symbol. Thus the owl says, "Words don't have meanings, people have meanings" and "Whatever you say a thing is, it isn't."

When navigating, the owl is always aware of the imperfect correspondence between maps and territories. Reality is dynamic, and yet our vocabularies change slowly, if at all. Processes and events take place simultaneously, and yet language is sequential; words come from a speaker's mouth or a writer's pen, one at a time. In reality, no two things are exactly alike. Language, however, is finite, and so we are forced to use a limited number of words to describe an unlimited number of things. Failure to recognize these fundamental distinctions inevitably leads to confusion and misunderstanding.

The owlish navigator is fully aware that no single map can represent all the characteristics of a territory. This principle holds across all reaches of human knowledge. The mistake we make is to believe that our personal maps are complete and accurate. In fact, they are neither. Knowing this, the owl conducts his relationships with tolerance and humility.

As all experienced travelers know, navigation is best accomplished by using a variety of maps drawn from different projections. Thus the owl cross-checks his knowledge by using a variety of different perspectives, gradually assembling a more complete and accurate picture.

Territories change. Bridges wash out, roads are rerouted, buildings are torn down and rebuilt. Personal territories also change. Consequently, our language maps also need to be updated periodically. Unfortunately, most of us walk around with outdated language maps, wondering why it is sometimes difficult to find our way. It is no wonder that we become frustrated and lost.

If there is a discrepancy between the map and the territory, it is *always* the map that is in error. The territory can never be wrong. If there is a difference between your words and the things that you are trying to describe, it is your words that must be adjusted. For most of us, this is an extremely difficult lesson to learn. We create maps of the world and then curse the territory for being wrong. How much easier it would be if we simply revised our personal maps to reflect the territory as it is revealed to us.

Do not neglect this lesson. Look for the territory at all times. Look for meanings in people, not in the words they happen to choose. Do not be distracted by superficial sounds and symbols. Listen to the unexpressed language; the meaning and intent that lies behind, between, and around the words. Update your maps frequently. Change your words to fit the territory. Throw out the erroneous, irrelevant, or inaccurate symbols and replace them with symbols that are more nearly correct.

Once you understand the relationship between maps and territories, you will no longer be a slave to language. Instead of worshiping words or reacting compulsively to them, you can look to the territory they represent. Your perceptions become much clearer as you begin to look at the territory itself. You will be less vulnerable to misunderstanding and your artistry at all levels will improve.

Take inspiration from the owlish navigator Chuang Tzu:

The fish trap exists because of the fish; once you've gotten the fish, you can forget the trap. The rabbit snare exists because of the rabbit; once you've got the rabbit, you can forget the snare.

Once you know the territory, you can forget the map. Once you've got the meaning, you can forget the words.

Mind Your Metaphors

The key instrument of the creative imagination is analogy.

E. O. Wilson

Human beings are analogical animals; we explore the unknown by probing it with images of the known. We use metaphor to transfer meaning from one domain to another and create connections between distant points, weaving them into a single integrated structure. What we call "understanding" usually means finding a metaphor that connects the unfamiliar with the familiar.

The fledgling dismisses metaphor as mere figure of speech, but the owl knows better. Subtly and powerfully, metaphor directs our attention and constructs our worldviews. In many ways, the metaphor *is* the message. If we say that two people are "sparring" with each other over an idea, we get one perspective. If we say that they are "brainstorming," we get an entirely different image. If we say that commerce is like "war," we look for behaviors such as aggression and defense. If we say that commerce is like "fishing," we think about skill, patience, and the elusive "big one."

Conflict often begins with metaphorical mismatch. If I see our relationship as a "wrestling match" and you see it as a "waltz," we are bound to get into trouble. If I see the human predicament as "dog-eat-dog" and you see it as a "lifeboat," we will probably disagree on the best way to build a future.

Thus the owl questions his metaphorical environment. Listen for the word bridges that connect domains. Listen to the metaphors that your opponent chooses. Once you discover his metaphorical inclination, you will understand his understanding. You may not happen to like his choice of analogy, but at least you will be able to communicate.

Do not accept metaphor mindlessly. Search for quality. Poor metaphors perpetuate associations that are stagnant, superficial, or destructive. Rich metaphors drive our insight deeper and explore connections that lead to yet more connections.

Listen carefully. Many metaphors are so thoroughly embedded in our sentences that they are nearly invisible. Do you recognize the metaphorical message in "a body of water"? "the bloodstream"? "the face of the mountain"?

Metaphorical flexibility is essential but demanding. It requires that we make fundamental, sometimes drastic shifts in perspective. If you have always looked on human society as a "machine" or a "rat-race," it may be difficult to see it as an "organism" or a "family." If you have always seen marriage as a "duel" with an occasional "truce," it may be difficult to see it as a "dance." You may have to totally restructure your worldview to accommodate these new perspectives. Be prepared for this possibility.

If you don't like the metaphors that are currently in use, invent new ones. Create word bridges between any two domains that you choose. You are not required to speak or perceive through any particular set of metaphors. You are not required to use combat metaphors to describe political campaigns, legal practice, or business. You can just as easily draw metaphors from gardening, fishing, or music. Choose metaphors that lead away from destructive confrontation and toward ecological relationship. Develop a rich repertoire of metaphorical language and use it with awareness and flexibility.

Master Abstraction

> The interesting writer, the informative speaker, and the accurate thinker operate on all levels of the abstraction ladder, moving quickly and gracefully from higher to lower, from lower to higher, with minds as lithe and deft and beautiful as birds on the wing.
>
> Adapted from S. I. Hayakawa, *Language in Thought and Action*

As a language artist, the owl is highly sensitive to abstraction, the process by which we move our attention from the palpable to the intangible.

At the lowest level of abstraction are material objects that we can see and touch. Here we are in close sensory contact with the things we are talking about. At this level, there is a high likelihood of agreement. If you are talking about a rock, I have a pretty clear idea of what you are referring to. We have both seen rocks with our own eyes, so there is not a great deal to argue about. If we disagree on the nature of a rock, we can go and observe one.

When we discuss high-level abstractions, however, we deal with things that are remote from our senses. We cannot touch "evolution" or taste "wealth." We cannot put our hands on "idealism." We cannot hear or smell "education." Since we can't experience these things directly, it is exceedingly difficult to agree on what they actually mean.

High-level abstractions give us great leverage, but like all powerful technologies, they allow us to make tremendous errors. You can't go too far wrong if you're talking about trees, bricks, and horseshoes, but if you start talking about "virtue," "spirituality," or "consciousness," you can get in trouble in a hurry.

People naturally have different appetites for abstraction. Some like to keep things down to earth, while others prefer to fly in the stratosphere of refined speculation. Neither level is good in and of itself. What is good is cyclic movement from the low to the high and back again. What is bad is the inability to move between the high and the low. Abstraction that festers on a single level is stagnant and therefore lifeless.

Owlish conversation begins with particulars, moves to generalization, and then moves back again. Don't get stuck on one level; mix it up. If you are lost in the clouds, get back to earth—tangible reality and specific cases. If you are tired of the trees and brush, ride the thermals back into the sky and search for powerful generalities.

If we would simply take the time to get our conversations aligned to the same levels of abstraction, we would all be much better off. Most fledglings are far too careless with this. They toss abstractions around as if everyone knows what they are talking about. They assume that everyone knows what they mean when they say "moral," or "existential," or "values." By using these words carelessly, the fledgling sows the seeds of conflict.

Bring your conversation down to a lower level of abstraction. Define your terms. Question definitions before leaping into the fray. If argument begins, look for the referent, the "thing itself" that people are arguing about. If you can get the level of abstraction low enough, all parties should eventually agree on something. Once you reach this point, you can venture back up into higher levels of speculation and perhaps more fruitful discussion.

Keep the Dialogue Moving

Discussion is an exchange of knowledge;
argument an exchange of ignorance.

Robert Quillen

One of the most direct paths to ecological relationship is dialogue. This is a special form of conversation with a unique spirit. The objective is to expand intelligence, refine ideas, discover new knowledge, and create options.

Dialogue is not debate. A debate is an intellectual competition between opposing points of view in which each side's perspective is exactly opposed by the other; the issue is perfectly polarized. Thus, the spirit of debate is adversarial and combative. The objective, of course, is victory.

Debate can be a useful training exercise, but as a means for developing ecological relationship or resolving conflict, it fails spectacularly. Since it is intentionally structured in black and white, it actually amplifies conflict and inhibits discussion of any alternatives between or beyond the extremes. Debate hardens positions that might otherwise have been flexible and often ends in deadlock.

In a debate, participants are expected to defend and advance their positions. Changes in perspective are viewed as weakness; the person who yields is considered a poor debater. This is precisely the problem. In the context of human learning and education, changing and refining one's views is the essence of intelligence. In debate, however, players are encouraged to fix their ideas and secure them against revision. In this sense, debate encourages intellectual rigidity, dogma, and social chaos.

In contrast, dialogue is characterized by the willingness to discard erroneous ideas and misconceptions. Each party may revise their viewpoints or adopt those of the other. Dialogue is thus a creative, evolutionary process. When well executed, it creates a synthesis of ideas in which the whole is greater than the sum of its parts. A dialogue may reach a tentative conclusion for action, but it is fundamentally open-ended; it can be resumed at any time.

Dialogue begins with the ability to listen. The fledgling thinks she knows this already, but if she really paid attention to her mind in conversation, she would discover that she is scarcely listening at all. Instead, she is composing her thoughts in preparation for the moment when her partner stops talking. As soon as he pauses for breath, the fledgling seizes the opening and presents her own point of view. When two fledglings talk to one another, the result is a double monologue.

In contrast, the owl's listening mind is open, yielding, and receptive; it is yin. Empty your mind of random thoughts and noise that will interfere with understanding. Hold no attitude. Suspend criticism and judgment, even if what your partner says is misinformed nonsense. Listen from the place of perfect ignorance, never assuming that you know anything at all.

When the fledgling "listens," she reacts. She looks at the speaker, decides whether she likes him or not, and then evaluates his statements on that basis. If she happens to like the speaker's appearance, ideology, or attitude, she accepts whatever he has to say. If she dislikes his appearance, ideology, or attitude, she rejects his statements. Her mind does not distinguish between the message and the messenger.

The owl is more sophisticated in her listening artistry. She observes the speaker to be sure, but evaluates his statements on their merits. She can accept the speaker and reject his statement, or she can reject the speaker and accept his statement. The owl does not get swept up by mere image or allow likes and dislikes to close her mind. Her objective is intelligence. She wants creative ideas and is not particularly concerned about where they come from. Her worst enemy could be, and often is, the source of creative inspiration. Thus she embraces the raw message.

Once the owl has listened attentively, he reviews his understanding. Unfortunately, many of us skip this step entirely as we rush to voice our opinions, and the dialogue rapidly degenerates into confusion, nonsense, or anger. If you doubt the quality of your understanding, stop the flow of conversation and probe for greater clarity. Be assertive in this effort. Have your partner deliver his message again and clarify it if need be. Ask dumb questions. Do not build a conversational castle on a foundation of sand. The fledgling thinks that asking for clarification makes her sound stupid, but this is actually an act of respect and intelligence.

Of course, there is more to conversation than just listening and talking. The fledgling feels obliged to keep her tongue in motion, but the owl is under no such compulsion; he relishes the space between the words. Silence allows a conversation to reverberate; it nurtures understanding and tempers the rush to react. Silence can also be an effective form of nonresistance, a yin stroke. The fledgling associates silence with weakness and defeat, but the owl knows its power. How can the debater attack your position if you say nothing? In many cases, power comes not from what you say, but from the silence that you keep. Use your silence like a second language.

A dialogue is a fragile process that can go astray at any moment. Emotions may flare up or you may become lost in confusion or revision. Or you may become defensive and try to secure your ideas against challenges. In any event, remain fluid. The spirit of collaboration, of shared searching, is the key. Even if you manage to dialogue only for a few moments, you will have strengthened the relationship and advanced your understanding. If you find the dialogue degenerating, take time out and then try again. If a debater attacks your position, treat the attack as irrelevant and continue your search for truth and insight. Be persistent. The spirit of dialogue is often contagious.

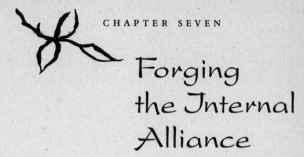

CHAPTER SEVEN

Forging the Internal Alliance

Integrate

> If I concentrate while he divides, I can use my
> entire strength to attack a fraction of his.
>
> Sun Tzu

There is one master principle of combat and conflicted relationship that every aspiring owl must know: If all other things are equal, the side that is more unified will win. This principle holds at all levels, from simple verbal disputes to full-scale battlefield engagements. The more "at one" you are, the better your chances for effective performance. Integration contributes to victory, dis-integration to defeat.

Given this general principle, the owl's first objective is to unite his powers into a single synchronized unit. At this level, the owl practices a yoga that connects his forces into a physical, mental, and spiritual whole.

This is an internal approach to martial artistry. The locus of attention is on self, not on the opponent. In striving for integration, the owl attends to his own personal spirit, posture, and behavior. The opponent is, in a significant way, irrelevant.

Personal integrity should always be secured before taking external action. Incredibly, many fledglings do precisely the opposite. Instead of cultivating internal cohesion, they attack impulsively. This is a fundamental error. By acting externally, without a foundation of integration, the fledgling uses only a fraction of his strength and is thus extremely vulnerable. The owl, on the other hand, deepens his personal and somatic integration. He refuses to allow his opponent to distract him from his integrative efforts.

Instead of going to pieces as stress intensifies, the owl harnesses the dissonance of conflict to power his integration even more completely. This is a counterintuitive approach. If a relationship becomes ambiguous or an opponent turns up the heat, turn your mind around. Use the stress as a paradoxical stimulus for your own integration. Use the pressure of conflict to drive your mind-body together. When your adversary shouts, screams, and threatens, change your psychic polarity and integrate more completely.

Adjust your posture. Attend to your breath. Focus on your objectives. Your explicit goals will help you channel the multiple aspects of personality into a whole.

Fire your imagination with images of integration. Picture a circle, a sphere, or a galaxy with powerful centripetal forces. Inspire the attractive forces within you. Your adversary can try his best, but his strikes will be ineffective. The more vigorously he attacks, the more united your forces become.

Promote integration by attending to the details of your daily life. Integrate by habit. Do not allow your attention to fragment into a multitude of separate tracks that tear you in different directions. Whenever possible, do one thing at a time. When walking, walk. When reading, read. When eating, eat. The ability to perform multiple tasks at the same time is impressive and sometimes useful, but there is also great power in doing single tasks to completion. The more often you create a sense of integration in your daily life, the easier it will be to drop into it on demand.

If personal integration is not enough to defend yourself or resolve a conflict, you may attempt to divide your opponent's forces. This is an advanced approach that is more appropriate for crisis situations. Here you will look for your opponent's weaknesses and exploit them as thoroughly as possible. Find a gap and drive a wedge into it.

In all cases, however, maintain your integration. Remember, striking an opponent will invariably create openings in your own forces. Do not over-commit to external action; the extreme may lead to its opposite. If your gut tells you that danger is increasing or that you are vulnerable, withdraw and reestablish your sense of integration. When in doubt, integrate.

Embrace the Fear Animal

The man who has ceased to fear has ceased to care.

F. H. Bradley

A good scare is worth more than good advice.

Edgar Watson Howe

Fear is one of the great cybernetic regulators. In small amounts, it focuses attention and prepares the body for action. It alerts us to possible danger and so keeps us alive. When fear grows too great, however, it becomes toxic and pollutes the entire psychophysical ecosystem. It shrinks our intelligence, fragments our attention, destroys our rationality, and compromises our balance. When gripped by fear, we fall back on fixed reaction patterns and dualistic thinking.

Unfamiliar and intimidated by the fear animal, the fledgling strives for fear-free existence; he tries to master it, drive it out, or run away from it. Fear becomes yet another adversary and his mind becomes divided against his body. In opposing his fear, he fails to hear the vital messages and warnings that it provides. He loses his sensitivity.

For the owl, on the other hand, fear is a welcome and essential ally. Fear speaks to him through his deep body intuition and gives advanced warnings of potential dangers. Thus his mind and body become integrated and his overall performance improves dramatically.

There are two possible errors that you can make in your fear relationship. The first is to be afraid of situations, people, or things that are not really dangerous. This is a misinterpretation of reality and a waste of valuable psychic energy. As you fixate on phantom dangers and illusory challenges, you simultaneously omit genuine dangers and opportunities; this makes you vulnerable and ineffective. By being afraid of the wrong person or situation, your relationships will become distorted. Your misplaced fear may actually inspire the kind of behavior that you were afraid of in the first place. Nothing inspires conflict so quickly and surely as paranoia. If you are going to be afraid of something, at least let it be something that is genuinely dangerous.

The complementary error is to *not* be afraid of genuine dangers. Obviously, this omission puts you at tremendous risk, and you are bound to stumble into accident and injury. These events will seem random and unprovoked, but they will really be the result of your failure to recognize danger in the first place.

The solution lies in congruence. Hone your fear through observation and study. Question your predicament. How dangerous *are* bears, anyway? What are the chances of being killed by lightning? What is the risk of losing your job or going out of business? What do people really die of? Should you be more afraid of a random mugging or domestic violence? Look for true risk. Base your fears on real challenges, real threats, real possibilities. Fine-tune your fear to correspond to reality; make your fear meaningful. Be afraid of the right things at the right time and in the right degree.

In training for performance in your chosen discipline, challenge yourself gradually and give your mind-body time to adapt; view your fear from a distance. Gradual immersion is the key. Become familiar with the process a little at a time, find out what your capabilities are, and learn what makes your fear animal tick.

As always, preemption is power. Don't get hooked into the positive feedback spiral of escalating fear in the first place. Keep breathing. Listen to fear's first whisper when it warns of impending danger—don't wait for it to start yelling. By then it will be too late.

Trust Your Gut

When the fledgling faces a tough decision, he often gets a hunch, a nagging feeling in his deep body that tells him what to say or do. Unfortunately, he is too busy calculating to listen. Convinced that his conscious mind is his best and only ally, he analyzes, worries, and reviews every aspect of his predicament and makes his decision on what he considers to be carefully considered reason. Later, when his decision turns out to be wildly wrong, he curses and grits his teeth in frustration.

The owl has had this experience too, but he has extracted a lesson from it. Instead of ignoring the wisdom of his deep body, he listens carefully and cultivates a harmonious, ecological relationship.

This trusting relationship is vital in high-stress encounters, especially in hand-to-hand self-defense. Here the conscious mind does not have time to function. By the time we think to block or punch, the opportunity for decisive action is gone. Fortunately, the body is often smarter than we are and knows precisely what to do.

The owl finds tremendous advantage in listening to his deep body. The somatic core is in intimate contact with our evolutionary heritage and all life on earth. It is enormously sensitive to survival and self-preservation. It speaks the language of the nonverbal universe and gives access to oceanic insight, a broad sense of intelligence. In many cases, the deep body knows when to push back and when to yield, when to go for it and when to go with it.

The conscious, rational mind is impressive in the way that it can categorize and manipulate symbols, but it is nevertheless a fragment of your total power. To rely exclusively on your rational mind is like using just one of your arms to engage the world. Better to use your entire body for integrated movement and action.

The deep body is like a child prodigy that needs guidance to shape its power. Thus the owl begins with discipline and proceeds by progressive withdrawal of conscious control as skills improve. Start your practice with perfect form, proper sequence, and methodical execution. Never practice more rapidly than the tempo at which you can proceed without hesitation and error. Once you achieve competence at this level, relax your conscious grasp slightly and allow the deep body to fill the gap. Relinquish control in a spiral fashion, a little at a time.

If your discipline is tight at the beginning and your withdrawal slow and progressive, the deep body will eventually be able to take over more and more of your performance. This will expand your abilities significantly. As you become increasingly skilled, you will be able to allow the deep body more influence and a greater voice in your behavior.

Practice this adjustment frequently. Tighten and relinquish conscious control one degree at a time. As your skills improve, you can give the deep body a chance to prove itself. When faced with a dilemma or a tough decision, don't react, but listen for the first impulses and words that emerge from the deep body. You need not act on them right away or without question, but take note. Acknowledge their existence.

The deep body is not infallible, of course, and there will be times when listening to your gut will take you in the wrong direction. This, however, is a chance that you must take. Refusal to listen to your deep body will lead to even more grievous errors or, at best, a stifled and stagnant existence of internal noise and tension. If you never give the deep body a chance to express itself, its voice will grow weaker and less assertive. Or it will subvert your conscious rationality and erode your ability to think clearly.

Of course, the owl does not discard his intellectual capabilities entirely or attempt to rely on his deep body alone. There is a difference between listening to the deep body and simply doing what happens to feel good at the time. The fledgling cannot trust his deep body because he has no training and no experience in adjusting his conscious control; most of his untrained impulses lead only to instant gratification. The owl can trust his gut because his deep body wisdom springs from disciplined practice.

Do not be misled. The conscious mind serves a perfectly useful and valid survival function. Take an integrated approach. In the beginning, discipline must assume control, but as the relationship matures, it becomes a dialogue where each aspect listens to and honors the other.

Do what you can with consciousness; calculate, reason, and analyze. Then, when this resource reaches its limit, turn back and yield to the unconscious and the irrational power of the deep body. Let that power express itself. Treat the deep body as a deep ally. Listen to its opinions and trust them.

Let the Darkness Be

There is a schizophrenia within all of us. There
are times that all of us know somehow there is a
Mr. Hyde and a Dr. Jekyll in us.

Martin Luther King, Jr.

For many of us, our most compelling conflict lies not with some external adversary, but with the dark "other" within ourselves. Ideally, we
would like to make this relationship functional, creative and whole. As
Gregory Bateson put it, we are looking for "an ecology of mind."

Recognizing this, our objective is extremely paradoxical. On the
one hand, we seek a sense of unity, wholeness, integration. At the same
time, we must honor the ecological value of opposition and resistance.
Without some internal tension, we would have no psychic energy, no
motivation, no creativity. A perfectly harmonious internal environment would be static and sterile. Of course, excess opposition can also
lead to diminishing returns and eventual self-defeat. Thus the art is to
find the optimal level of psychic and spiritual opposition. The dose
makes the medicine.

The ideal state is characterized by both opposition and harmony.
With this in mind, the owl imagines the internal other as an ecological
enemy. This opposing "other" provides the necessary psychic resistance
to stimulate growth and creativity, but only in service of the system as a
whole. In this sense, the internal other is an ally, even in its opposition.

Think of the internal other as a talented and benevolent sparring
partner, a creative personality that keeps you attentive and honest. Carl
Jung described the ideal relationship this way:

Conscious and unconscious do not make a whole when one of them is suppressed and injured by the other. If they must contend, let it at least be a fair fight with equal rights on both sides. Consciousness should defend its reason and protect itself, and the chaotic life of the unconscious should be given the chance of having its way too—as much as we can stand. This means open conflict and open collaboration at once.

The dynamic of internal relationship is identical to the hand-to-hand encounter at the double-hinged door. If you respond push for push, you set up a symmetrical, adversarial relationship. Your attempts to suppress, contain, pin, or otherwise silence the internal other will probably fail.

The superior strategy is to complement the challenge of the internal other. Here the owl yields to the push and allows the internal other its due expression. In this way, it fails to build up power through symmetrical escalation.

Of course, the owl does not give the internal other free rein to push as far as it likes, nor does she allow herself to be victimized. She asserts her power and interests just as she would in any other relationship. She sets limits, but yields intelligently to give the shadow its chance for expression.

Sensei Jung described the internal other as "the shadow," a powerful psychic force, simultaneously the source of our most frightening and most creative impulses. The fledgling, of course, feels uncomfortable with his primal urges and motivations. If the shadow generates a desire to howl at the moon or assault a relative or a colleague, his first impulse is to force it back down into the depths of unconsciousness. If he is ever questioned about such impulses, he may even deny that they exist.

In order to become functioning members of a community, we must, to a certain extent, tame the shadow. We cannot allow every unconscious impulse to express itself at will. But in our quest to tame the shadow, we risk creating yet another adversarial relationship. When the shadow is the enemy, we are moved to destroy it, which is to say, we declare war with ourselves.

The shadow does not yield easily to suppression or the use of force. Like many enemies, it actually thrives on resistance. When we try to repress the shadow, it often grows stronger, which motivates us to repress it that much more vigorously. Clearly, there is little future in this kind of relationship.

If the fledgling is unsuccessful at repressing her dark side, she may project it out into the world around her. Instead of acknowledging her own tendencies toward violence, greed, and lust, she unconsciously projects them into the social ecosystem; she keeps the "good" inside and the "bad" outside. Now the cause of her anxiety appears to lie outside herself, and she achieves a measure of psychological security.

Unfortunately, this is a dangerous illusion that puts her in a psychological hall of mirrors. Shadow projection only exaggerates and deepens conflict, which leads to more internal strife, which leads to more projection, more distortion, and more conflict. Ultimately, the fledgling ends up reacting to her own projections.

The only solution to this tendency is vigilant attention. Strive for unbiased disinterest. Look within and suspend judgment. See people, organizations, and cultures as they truly are, not through the haze of your psychological experience. Wield a realistic, objective approach of unprejudiced observation and revision.

Acknowledging the shadow requires that we accept the dark side of our human nature. The fledgling denies that she could commit violence, betray others, or live a life of deceit, but the shadow lies in all human beings and in every human culture; every person who has ever lived has the potential for darkness and evil.

Maintain a healthy relationship with your shadow by living the phrase, "Anything a human being can do, I can do." This includes *all* human behaviors and abilities, from the most heroic to the most heinous. If a human being can heal the sick, you have that potential; if a human being can build a prisoner-of-war camp and torture the captives, you have that potential as well. We all have the capacity for depravity as well as artistry.

Maintain an ecological shadow relationship by developing a strong and vigorous personality; use one aspect of the psyche to counterbalance the other. Nurture this balance with expertise in your chosen art or discipline. Competence leads to security and greater assurance in facing the shadow within.

Integrating the shadow is not a one-time, all-or-nothing proposition. It is not as if we could say, "Yes, I have a dark side" and be done with it. Shadow integration and projection awareness are a continuous challenge. Thus the owl turns her gaze inward regularly and rhythmically, in a search for her true motivations. She asks: Is my boss really an aggressive and insensitive scoundrel? Are my neighbors really criminal? Or am I simply seeing my shadow?

In his polarized world, the fledgling spends his time fleeing the dark and running toward the light, oblivious to the fact that contrast is necessary for vision. But in order to make peace with the shadow, we must learn to dwell in the same house with the dragon. Instead of constantly seeking enlightenment, turn your mind around. Seek instead a sense of endarkenment, an appreciation for the shadows in life, the places where the light does not penetrate. Without darkness, after all, the light would be meaningless.

Let the darkness be.

CHAPTER EIGHT

A Glimpse of Wisdom

Twice or thrice the young bird may be deceived, but before the eyes of the full-fledged it is vain to spread the net, or speed the arrow.

DANTE ALIGHIERI

Embrace Vulnerability

When she is young, the owlet experiences the forces of nature as awesome and totally beyond her control. She struggles as best she can and relies on others for support and sustenance. Later, she begins to feel a sense of competence as she succeeds in protecting herself from the dangers of her physical and social environment.

This, paradoxically, is a point of extreme danger. On the one hand, the owlet feels the confidence to handle increasingly difficult challenges. On the other, she begins to harbor the illusion that she is immune to harm; she may even begin to feel invulnerable.

In this process, familiarity breeds complacency. The fledgling says, "This is an ordinary moment. This pattern is familiar and predictable. I can relax." At this point, her mind becomes blind to novelty. She stops scanning, stops asking questions, and becomes oblivious to genuine risk.

As usual, the extreme leads to its opposite. As soon as we imagine that we are untouchable by the forces of the physical and social environment, we sabotage our intelligence. The relationship is an inverse one. The more invulnerable we feel, the more vulnerable we are likely to be.

The way of the owl, therefore, is to continuously acknowledge vulnerability across all realms. Even as you become experienced, comfortable, and masterful in your position and discipline, remain aware of the possibilities for accident and error. Honor the unpredictable and keep your fallibility firmly in mind.

On the battlefield of life, there are a million more ways to get thrown than you can possibly prepare for. You can study the ways of hand-to-hand combat and be reasonably safe on the street, but then get struck by lightning. You can achieve financial security and then fall victim to poor health. The universe is too complex and too dynamic for any individual or group to achieve total security. There are always weaknesses that can be exploited by a clever or lucky opponent. For every strategy, there is a counter; rock smashes scissors, scissors cuts paper, paper covers rock.

As is so often the case, safety lies not in more defense, but in less. Expose yourself to *all* possibilities, pleasant and unpleasant alike. Embrace the possibility of error, failure, injury, suffering, and death. This acceptance will keep your mind open and alert.

The quest for invulnerability is seductive but ultimately self-defeating. The fledgling who believes he is invulnerable becomes lax and inattentive. Breaks in his attention provide opportunities for opponents to strike. Thus the saying of the classical martial artist: "Believing that you are invulnerable is the ultimate vulnerability."

Not only is invulnerability impossible, it is also undesirable. To be invulnerable is to be isolated, separated, and therefore alienated from the rest of the world. An invulnerable warrior could not participate in the friendly aspects of the universe; to strive for complete security is to strive for disconnection and loneliness.

No matter how great your skill becomes, never allow yourself to believe that you are immune to attack, error, accident, or misfortune. There is no invulnerability in this universe. Disciplined training only improves the odds.

See the Humor

Have you heard the story of the French general?
When his army became surrounded, he
exclaimed "Wonderful! This means we can
attack in any direction!"

Anonymous

Some imagine the master conflict artist as a grim, scowling warrior, ever-ready to suffer and die in battle. In fact, the true owl is coyote-like in her attention and behavior, a trickster with a taste for mischief. She has a keen sense of the absurd, the incongruous, and the hysterical. She takes delight in her ability to recombine parts of her experience into paradoxical and far-fetched combinations.

Humor stimulates the owl's creativity at all levels. It helps her to explore unlikely connections between categories and leapfrog out of established patterns and ruts. Jokes scramble the literal and the metaphorical, stimulate lateral thinking, generate new options and force us to make drastic shifts in perspective. Laughter stimulates breathing and promotes animal health.

The power of humor lies in the way that it changes context and perspective. Humor is a step outside, an alternative vision. When wielded with skill, it can be far more powerful than an avalanche of logic or reason.

Humor disarms nervous minds and brings down the temperature of conflicted relationship. It breaks down tensions, reduces anxiety, and stimulates dialogue. Laughter makes us receptive; it reduces pressure on the door of conflict.

A taste for humor also helps the owl maintain a sense of proportion and prevents her from becoming a true believer, a zealot who thinks that her way is the only way. The true believer is so engrossed in herself and her cause that she loses her sense of perspective and becomes rigid, dogmatic, and intolerant; she claims that all other paths are misguided, irrelevant, or evil. The owl, on the other hand, appreciates the absurdity of things, including her own efforts. Thus she remains balanced and effective.

Owlish humor is not mere wit or cleverness. Rather, it is a sophisticated sense of ironic insight that blends with the curious and intriguing nature of the universe. This is a celebration of life, a deep and provocative study in its own right.

Owlish humor is a function of attention; a discipline that can be learned. When pushed through cyclic yang-yin effort, it becomes more acute. If neglected, it atrophies. Use the hilarious or lose it.

Sensitize yourself to humor in all its forms. Hone your sense of the ridiculous. Study the creations of the masters and practice at every opportunity. Mix and match the various aspects of your experience into plausible but hilarious combinations. Use exaggeration and understatement to explore limits and demolish static reality. Use irony to challenge assumptions and entrenched worldviews. Cross boundaries and build bridges between things that have no apparent relationship.

Take humor seriously. Expand your comic consciousness. Open your mind to the absurd and paradoxical; look for the joker in the deck. Savor the tricks of the universe. Use humor preemptively to build relationship and use it when you are stuck to generate new alternatives. Ambush your comrades and adversaries with jokes of all varieties. When faced with stubborn resistance, don't get even, get odd. Harness the humor to free your mind.

Embrace Ambiguity, Risk, and Paradox

The painter who has no doubts will achieve little.

Leonardo da Vinci

The test of a first-rate intelligence is the ability to hold two opposed ideas in mind at the same time and still function.

F. Scott Fitzgerald

If human lives and relationships are anything, they are complex, over-lapping, multidimensional, and nonlinear. They are ambiguous and dynamic, filled with an astonishing variety of roles, meanings, intents, and purposes. A person, a group, or a process may be in hundreds of different pigeonholes all at the same time.

In this ever-changing environment, ambiguity tolerance is the key factor that allows the owl to maintain his psychophysical performance. He knows how to live in the midst of uncertainty and doubt without compulsively groping after rationality and security. Since he can tolerate dissonance, he can keep his mind open when the heat is rising and things are disintegrating all around. This has practical advantages: Since his mind can stay open just a little bit longer, he is likely to see an opening or option that leads him to safety. At the same time, his superior ambiguity tolerance contributes to peaceful and civilized relation-ship. Since he can tolerate the fuzziness and doubt that comes with a conflicted relationship, he is less inclined to reach for quick fixes or "military solutions."

The fledgling's poor ambiguity tolerance makes him impulsive and highly reactive. Uncomfortable with the dissonance of conflict, he reaches for black-and-white solutions that ultimately make things worse. As his stress level increases, he gropes for any quick resolutio 1, whether it has any real merit or not. Ultimately, his demand for security actually precipitates conflict and friction in otherwise healthy relationships. By trying to slay the dragons of ambiguity, doubt, and insecurity, the fledgling actually creates more of them.

The owl is in no great hurry to impose order on situations and relationships. He knows the art of delayed gratification. Even as he feels the storm of negative emotion that comes with polarization, he tries to live with it a little longer; this is yin. Even if he can only buy a few moments or hours, he will gain some valuable opportunity. Make this a global practice; any experience in delayed gratification is valuable.

Life is an inherently high-risk enterprise. There is no ultimate security in the game of rock-scissors-paper. Whether you are looking for self-defense, victory, or a peaceful and equitable solution, you will have to face some degree of danger. The most effective solutions to conflict—adaptation, conciliation, disarmament, compromise, graduated responses—also make us vulnerable. Risk-free conflict solutions are a myth. If you harden your position to defend yourself against risk, you put fear into your opponents, which puts you at greater risk. Thus *not* risking may actually be the greatest risk of all.

Because of his limited experience, the fledgling dismisses the improbable as unworthy of serious consideration. But time amplifies the capricious quality of life; situations and relationships that would be improbable on any given day are almost certain to occur in the long run. The longer you live, the more you must prepare for the unusual and the unexpected. Thus the owlish warrior learns to expect nothing and prepares his mind for the unusual, the bizarre, and the impossible.

Hone your ambiguity tolerance on the stone of novelty. Make regular trips to the boundary of your comfort zone. Position yourself to be an awkward beginner in some new discipline and become familiar with the dissonance. Be secure in the knowledge that it pays to be a fledgling, at least from time to time.

Beware of Certitude

Those who have excessive faith in their ideas
are not well fitted to make discoveries.

Claude Bernard

An idea is something you have; an ideology
is something that has you.

Morris Berman

As you move closer to owlhood, you will gain confidence and find it easier to take action in stressful and challenging situations. In your success, however, you may find yourself going past the point of thoughtful reflection and into the realm of dogma and certainty. This is a dangerous mistake.

The fledgling associates mastery with absolute confidence and conviction, but this is an illusion. Mastery, like all living things, moves. It is dynamic. The moment we "achieve" certainty, we fall out of mastery. As soon as we declare something "true" or "perfect," we prevent its further refinement. As soon as we believe ourselves masters, we become fools.

Dogmatic certainty is a psychological overextension, much like the punch that goes beyond its normal range and leaves us vulnerable. As with so many things, the extreme leads to its opposite. Dogma is too rigid to accommodate the demands of a dynamic battle or environment. If you can't change your mind, you can't step laterally. When you hold a view too tightly, you are held by it as well.

Certainty not only stalls learning, it ignites and perpetuates unnecessary conflict. Dogma makes no concessions and tolerates no revisions. It is rigid and static—not a good way to approach the bargaining table, the street, or the battlefield. To be authentic, mastery must be accompanied by continuous acknowledgment of ignorance, vulnerability, and partial understanding.

Naturally, there is a season and a time for everything. There are times when the pure force of conviction is essential for creative performance and survival. When a furious assailant grabs you by the throat, your response must be one of zero doubt. Nevertheless, as a continuous intellectual posture, pure conviction defeats itself. If you find yourself holding an attitude, a belief, or an idea with absolute certainty, break the pattern and start asking questions. You are in danger of reversal.

Live the Low Life

In order to see birds it is necessary to become
a part of the silence.

Robert Lynd

He does not want to shine,
therefore he will be enlightened.
He does not want to be anything for himself,
therefore he becomes resplendent.
He does not lay claim to glory,
therefore he accomplishes works.
He does not seek excellence,
therefore he will be exalted.

Lao Tzu, *Tao te Ching*

To become more masterful, you must integrate the lessons of owlhood
into your daily experience. This art begins and ends with attention to
detail in the here and now.

Access this art with a simple principle: Treat difficult things as if
they were easy and easy things as if they were difficult. Treat walking
and sitting as if they were highly demanding activities that are crucial
to life and death. Treat cooking and eating as if they were the most
subtle and difficult of all arts. The fledgling finds this suggestion absurd, believing that it imposes an incredible burden on his life. In fact,
this is precisely the key to the owl's success.

In her quest for owlhood, the beginner strives for the highest possible performance. She struggles against error and pushes her way up
the learning curve, always in search of the most refined and sophisticated creations. This is an honorable path, but it often distracts us from
the supreme importance of the common and ordinary.

High performance is glamorous and exciting, but in many ways, irrelevant. Low performance is routine, commonplace, and absolutely vital. Standing, sitting, breathing, walking, and eating are what our lives are made of. The fledgling thinks that these things are easy and therefore meaningless, but the owl knows better.

The owl seeks high performance, of course, but she does it indirectly. Instead of flying straight to the highest point, she attends to the low, the common, and the routine. She learns to do simple things extremely well so that she can maintain her form even under extreme stress. Thus she is always fully prepared to account for her every action, even the most mundane and innocent.

Become a master of the fundamentals of living and return to them often. Aspire to great achievement, but do not forget the basic skills of your life and chosen discipline.

Do not worry about the attentions of others in this quest for low performance. Few will notice or appreciate your expertise in daily living, but this does not matter. As Nietzsche put it, "The higher we soar, the smaller we appear to those who cannot fly."

Expand Your Heart

I am large. I contain multitudes.

Walt Whitman, *Song of Myself*

Owlish mastery is expansive and compassionate. It is tolerant of human weakness and incompetence. It understands the inevitability of dissent and the ease with which conflict can break out. It appreciates how difficult it is to remain centered in the face of chaos. Thus the expansive heart accepts even the most pathetic fledgling efforts toward owlhood, especially if they are sincere.

There are practical benefits to this expanded embrace. The amount of opposition in your life is inversely proportional to the size of your heart. Having a bigger heart means having less outside, which means less resistance, fewer adversaries, and fewer battles to fight. The small-hearted fledgling keeps much outside and is always fighting the externals, but the great-hearted owl embraces much and many. If you have everything inside, there is nothing left to fight.

And besides, the bigger your heart, the more fun you can have. The more you can accept the foibles of those around you, the more you can connect with their inevitable brilliance.

Of course, you can't let everyone or everything into your heart. But you can work the margin. Open your heart a fraction at a time. Let in a few ideas, a few phrases, a few personalities, a few gestures, a few emotions. Then adjust to this new dimension. Later, you may want to let in a bit more, or even contract in a crisis, but that will come in its own time. The heart does not expand overnight. The membrane around your heart will be hardened or softened cell by cell, word by word, sentence by sentence, action by action. Every little gesture contributes to the expansion or the contraction. Observe these events and guide them gently.

Practice this art of acceptance. Absorb the resistance that you encounter and make it part of you. Reframe your perspective to include wider experience and greater diversity. As your skill increases, you can expand your heart further without increasing your risk or vulnerability. Do not neglect this art! Great skill with a small heart is no skill at all.

As you expand your heart, don't forget to include yourself, your history, and your dragons; don't keep yourself outside. Big compassion accepts itself and in this, resistance fades and peace becomes possible.

Face the Ultimate Adversary

> Forget the years; forget distinctions. Leap into
> the boundless and make it your home!
>
> Chuang Tzu

Of all the opponents that we will face, there is one that stands alone in power and influence. We can parry some of his assaults, but this opponent has the luxury of being arbitrary, and for this there is no defense. He may make a few probing jabs and then gradually drag us to the ground or he may appear suddenly and serve up the final blow without warning. There is no power that can defeat him, no strategy that can upset his balance. This is death, the ultimate adversary.

Fighting death is a paradoxical battle of the highest order. It is a battle we must fight, but one we will certainly lose. There is no escape from this predicament. It must be lived.

The first principle, as always, is to be a good animal. Fighting for life is the way of all creatures. When death steps into the ring, you must summon up your reserves of strength and endurance. Give no quarter. Put up the fiercest resistance possible. Scratch and claw with every fiber and every cell. Look the adversary in the face. Do not go gentle.

On this level, our resistance to death is honorable and ecological, but there is another dimension to this relationship. This is the existential battle we wage in anticipation of the encounter and in protest against our predicament. We labor long and hard against the fact that we will have to meet this opponent. We deny and we squirm. We resist the inevitable.

Unfortunately, this resistance saps our energy and erodes our performance. The more you fight your encounter with the ultimate adversary, the less effective you will be. The sooner you accept its in-evitability and your eventual defeat, the stronger you will become. Denying death is a waste of psychic power and energy. You can try to push the ultimate adversary away, but he will laugh in your face. His endurance is legendary.

Thus the owlish relationship to death is simultaneously furious re-sistance and open acceptance. Fight it when it attacks, but do not allow it to seize your mind in anticipation. To the extent that death captivates your attention, you are already dead, held in the grip of a static fixation and fear. Better to include it and become one with it.

This predicament seems onerous, but in fact, the ultimate adversary is also the ultimate teacher. It reminds us of our vulnerability and shows us how to fight the minor battles; with dignity, with attention, with commitment. For the owlish warrior, each minor battle is a re-hearsal for the ultimate encounter.

In waging this encounter with the ultimate adversary, it is essen-tial that you question your relationship with time. For some, each grain of sand that falls through the hourglass is a defeat, a moment lost in the battle to maintain life. This, however, is a fool's battle be-cause time is a completely overwhelming foe. Any attempt to gain victory over time will only lead to increased anxiety and weakness. Only by entering fully into the flow of time can you achieve a state of no-enemy.

Owlish power lies in participation and alliance with the natural world. The more you attempt to separate yourself from the living world, the more terrifying and incomprehensible your death will ap-pear. Instead, make yourself part of a larger whole; become one with the grand drama of life. Unite with the larger organism and you will cease to worry.

Live completely, die completely. The way of the owl is to fight and yield simultaneously. Defeat will come. The only question is how we will engage it. Will you suffer defeat with honor and dignity as a good animal?

The desire for immortality is a desire to be separate from the natural world. This, however, is not the way of power. Weave yourself into the waxings *and* the wanings of the living world. Live your life and experience your death with dignity and open eyes. The owl lives and dies with noble strength.

Reflection

Before long, you will forget the lessons of owlhood and go back to your old habits of relationship; you will get out of position, procrastinate, and push like a stubborn fool on the door of conflict. You will fix your ideas and neglect your scan. You will think in black and white and get trapped by language. You will react compulsively and symmetrically.

There is no escape from this. The art, after all, is long and broad and deep. The only solution is continuous inquiry and willingness. Tie your white belt around your waist and step onto the mat. After a few thousand falls, your belt will become soiled with the grit of your experience. As the years go by, its color will deepen to brown and then to black. Your owlish nature will deepen as well, but even this will be provisional. Continued training will strip away the outer fibers of your belt, returning it to its original color as the cycle comes full circle. Fledgling becomes owl, owl becomes fledgling, and so on in an endless cycle.

The opportunity for owlhood lies in every challenge. Grasp it when possible, but if you miss, fly to the next opportunity and try again. There will be no shortage of opportunities.

At times it will seem that the owl's voice is faint. And yet, if you listen carefully, you can hear it all around you. The owl lives in many creatures, in many acts, and in the fabric of nature herself. Look for it and acknowledge it whenever you catch a glimpse. With attention, you will begin to see it with ever greater clarity.

When you face competition and meet resistance, ask yourself, "What would the owl do?" Then listen for the owl's voice within.

Fighting Words: Acknowledgments

> *The war against war is going to be no holiday*
> *excursion or camping party.*
>
> WILLIAM JAMES

Writing a book about conflict artistry is like doing battle with a mysterious and highly skilled opponent. The concepts are powerful, elusive, and paradoxical. Exceptions abound. For every idea that appears to be true, an opposite lurks in the shadows, waiting to attack the slightest weakness. My objective was to pin the words to the page, but sometimes I was the one who was thrown, smashed to the ground by the weight of conflicting ideas and diverse philosophies. Even after the words were firmly printed on paper, I still had doubts; I was afraid they would somehow leap off the page, grab me in some devious new hold, and send me crashing to the mat.

Fortunately, I have not had to face this battle alone. Numerous allies have picked me up, brushed me off, and sent me back into the fray. First among my supporters has been my family, my owlish parents and my loving wife, Susan. I am, of course, eternally indebted to all of my martial art senseis for their powerful teachings: Rod Martin, Kurt Schnoor, Tom Read, Koichi Barrish, and Mark Bartosh. I also thank my owlish readers for their valuable insight and support: Sam and Beth Forencich, the Fahringer family, Jim Collins, George Thompson, Mike Levy, Sandy Schaff, Ann Elsbach, John Williams, Sam Kraut, Betsy Levy, Larry Ball, and Troy Corliss. Special thanks to my climbing partners and bodywork teachers, who expanded my comfort zone and helped me to become a better animal.

Thanks, too, to the professionals who teamed up with me to wage the last campaigns to get these observations of a lifetime into a lithe, compact book: my visionary agent, Hal Zina Bennett, who made the right moves; my editor, John Loudon, who saw the potential in its earliest stages and masterfully guided my fledgling efforts through many challenging revisions; assistant editor Karen Levine and editorial assistant Matthew Harray, who joined the fray at crucial junctures; my production editor, Rosana Francescato; my copy editor, Naomi Lucks; and the whole flock of publishing owls at Harper San Francisco.